W9-DIU-947

# THE CROSS AND THE COMMON MAN

HERMAN W. GOCKEL

# *THE CROSS AND*

# THE COMMON MAN

An Everyday Religion for Everyday People

CONCORDIA PUBLISHING HOUSE

SAINT LOUIS, MISSOURI

Copyright 1955 by
Concordia Publishing House
St. Louis, Missouri

Library of Congress Catalog Card No. 55-12190

MANUFACTURED IN THE UNITED STATES OF AMERICA

# PREFACE

As the title of this book suggests, it was written especially for the common man. The common man, in this instance, is one of the approximately 99 per cent of our population who have never attended a theological seminary or who have never made a technical study of the Christian religion.

In other words, this is a book for the nonprofessional inquirer into the Christian faith. Its approach is that, for instance, of a lawyer discussing a point of law with his physician friend, or that of a physician discussing a point of medicine with his lawyer neighbor. In either case, when the one speaks to the other about a technical point in his particular field, he will proceed from the premise that, *at the present point of contact*, the other is a "common man." Technical vocabularies will, therefore, no longer be used without explanations, and professional presuppositions will no longer be presupposed. Indeed, in many instances it will have to be a matter of starting from scratch.

So, too, when the church today speaks to the common man about religion. Perhaps never before in the modern Christian era has it been so necessary for the church to start once more from scratch in presenting its message to the world around it as in the middle of the twentieth century. Dr. W. A. Visser 't Hooft, General Secretary of the World Council of Churches, recently said: "Modern mass man is so far removed from the thought-world of the Bible that it is almost a miracle if he can still understand the kind of things the Bible talks about." In a nation in which more than eighty million people claim no formal association with the church and in which the average Sunday finds more than a hundred million failing to make use of the church's teaching ministry, it would be folly to assume that the average person today has more than a passing acquaintance with the Christian message.

The day is gone, if, indeed, it ever was here, when the church could bandy such clichés as "There's salvation in the blood" or "Jesus saves" in the hope that they would convert the uninformed and unregenerate. The sentence "There's salvation in the blood," if written above the entrance to the local Red Cross office, could be an appeal for blood donors; and the words, "Jesus saves," if lettered on the window of a bank, could mean that Christ is a model of thrift and economy. Until these words are placed against their proper background and into their proper context, they are utterly meaningless. In the following pages we have tried to place them into their God-intended context for the benefit of the common man.

We are not promising that what follows is as clear and simple as a Third Grade Reader. This book is written for adults. And it deals with some of the profoundest thoughts which have occupied the heart and mind of man. Self-evidently we have had to use many of the words in which these thoughts have previously been expressed. That means we have not been able to get away completely from a theological vocabulary. Which, of course, is not surprising. You wouldn't expect your lawyer to explain a point of law without using legal phrases, but you *would* expect him to use those phrases in a way that you could understand them.

That is what we have tried to do in the following chapters. Whenever we have quoted a somewhat obscure phrase or sentence from the Bible, we have followed it immediately with a modern paraphrase. Some of our quotations from the Scripture have been taken from J. B. Phillips' well-known *Letters to Young Churches*, which is a modern translation of the New Testament Epistles. References to such quotations are indicated by a capital "P," as, for instance, Romans 3:28. P.

We sincerely hope and ardently pray that the pages of this volume will give to the common man not only a clearer picture of the Cross of Christ but also a deeper and more abiding faith in its redeeming power.

THE AUTHOR

# CONTENTS

## I

## STARTING FROM SCRATCH

It was a hectic day in Hollywood. As if there were any *other* kind of day in Hollywood during a tight production schedule! We were sitting next to the cameraman, waiting for the light men to get their equipment into position, when a clear-eyed young actress in her early twenties sat down beside us and said:

"Pastor, I've heard you say again and again that Jesus died — and that, because He died, our sins have been forgiven. What I don't get is: what's the connection?"

"What's the connection?"

There are millions of people who are asking the same question, and asking it sincerely. Perhaps you are one of them. You've heard it said again and again that "Jesus died." You've heard it shouted from street corners, exclaimed over radios, emblazoned on billboards, flashed on neon lights, and printed in tracts and books and pamphlets of all descriptions. And you've been told that because Jesus died, "your sins have been forgiven."

But, like our young actress friend, what you "don't get" is "What's the connection?" What's the connection between the death of a man over nineteen hundred years ago and my sins? How could there conceivably be any connection between the two?

There have been hundreds, yes, thousands, of men down through the ages who have given their lives for a noble cause — who have gone into death to uphold a lofty principle. But who would say that because they died our sins have been forgiven? Who would say, for instance, that because Abraham Lincoln sacrificed his life upon the altar of devotion to his country, you and I have been made right with God?

On the surface, it would seem absurd to say that the death of any man a hundred or a thousand or two thousand years ago could have any bearing on your relationship to God today. It would seem the rankest kind of superstition to say that, because a certain person gave up his life in the dim and distant past, God was willing to forgive and to forget any wrong that you might do today. And it would seem to be a theology of goblins which insisted that, unless you associate yourself with that one man's death in a very real and specific way, you can have no hope either in this life or in the life to come.

And yet that is exactly what the Christian religion claims. That is exactly what the church has been proclaiming down through the centuries. And that is exactly what the church is saying to you today. There *is* a connection between the death of Jesus Christ — and you.

Just what that connection is, we hope to make clear in the pages of this book. And we hope to do so without the thees and thous which usually characterize the traditional treatment of this subject. If there is any connection between the Cross and the common man, that connection must surely be expressible in language which the common man can understand. If the Cross of Christ has any relevance to the ordinary man in his office or at his workbench, or to the ordinary woman in her home, that relevance can surely be put into words to which the ears of ordinary people have become accustomed.

This does not mean that the common man will always *agree* with the connection which the Christian religion establishes between the Cross of Christ and him. Indeed, it is quite possible that he will not agree. But it does mean that this relationship can be expressed in such a way that the common man can understand the language which is used. Having understood the language, it will still be up to him to accept or to reject what that language says.

We trust that the reader will not be discouraged if in the following pages we take (what may seem to him) a roundabout way to give him a meaningful view of the Cross of Christ. It just so happens that there is no other way of getting there. The Cross of Christ cannot be seen in its true perspective except from a certain point of vantage.

Come with us, then, on that tortuous journey down into the valley — from the bottom of which we shall be able to look up and see the Cross of Christ in its only true significance!

## II

## *THE WORM IN THE APPLE*

Any discussion of the Cross and the common man could start in one of two places. It could start with the Cross. Or it could start with the common man. We have chosen to start with the common man.

What kind of person is he? Is he essentially good or essentially bad? Is he on the way up or on the way down? Is he to be congratulated or commiserated? Is he building his own Utopia or is he pulling the world down in destruction around his ears? Does he have within himself the power to rise above his present self and to usher in an era of peace and harmony, of equity and justice? Can he bring his will into conformity with God's? Does he have the spiritual power to pull himself up by his own bootstraps — and to reach the level of spiritual life that God intended for him?

No one can say that the common man (and the un-common man, for that matter!) hasn't been trying. Here in America he has erected, paid for, and continues to support a system of public education such as the world has never seen before. He has woven a network of grammar schools, high schools, colleges, and universities which has reached and enveloped almost every city, town, and hamlet in the country. By his collective effort he has achieved a level of general enlightenment unprecedented in the history of the human race. By the sheer power of his intellect and ingenuity he has added knowledge to knowledge until the "miracle" of yesterday has become the commonplace of today — electricity, the telephone, the radio, television, travel by land, sea, and air, the combustion motor, electronics, and atomic power, to mention only a few of the wonders of our age.

If the common man of the year 1800, sweating behind his ox-drawn plow, could have been convinced that by the year 1950 the mind of man would have produced all the miracles which have become commonplace today, he would no doubt have predicted that the decade of 1950 to 1960 would be a decade of Utopian freedom — freedom from fear, freedom from want, freedom from worry.

How could a civilization unshackled from the serfdom of primitive technology be anything but free and happy? he would have reasoned. In the midst of plenty, how could men be anything but

honest? In the midst of abundance, how could men
be anything but generous? In the midst of leisure,
how could men be anything but helpful? In the
midst of an ever-mounting capacity for production,
how could men be anything but secure? Surely, in
a world of miracles there would be righteousness,
charity, peace, security.

Or *would* there?

Perhaps the common man of 150 years ago
would have stroked his jaw in wonderment if he
had been told that in the year 1950 America, the
land of miracles, had an annual crime bill of sixteen billion dollars — that every hour of every day
and every night it spent an unconscionable per-
centage of its national income for the prevention,
prosecution, and punishment of crime. He would
surely have found it difficult to believe that during
*each day* of a recent year there had been committed in this land of unprecedented enlightenment and unparalleled abundance a total of 5,157
major crimes, and that among these there were
34 murders, 1,115 burglaries, 143 robberies, 3,064
larcenies, 46 rapes, 540 automobile thefts, and 215
aggravated assaults. And he would have rubbed
his eyes in dismay if he had read that during the
middle decade of this century of miracles the Amer-
ican people spent nearly 350 billions of dollars on
the arts and implements of war!

The common man of 1800, pondering the immeasurable advances and advantages of the common man today, would surely be surprised to find the common man today just as envious, just as greedy, just as deceitful, just as lustful, just as discontented, dishonest, disrespectful, disobedient, rebellious, selfish, and hard to get along with as the common man of 1800.

He would be surprised, too, to find that all the sorrows, all the fears, frustrations, and disappointments which plagued his life are still here — despite the world of miracles in which we live. Indeed, he would find that the fears and frustrations of enlightened America today run wider and deeper than those of his day — that suicides are on the increase, that psychiatrists have more patients than they can handle, that beds and rooms in mental hospitals are at a premium.

If the world of 1800 seemed out of joint to him, what would he say of the world in the middle of the twentieth century — so blessed with general enlightenment! He would very probably say that the world must be possessed. And, indeed, he would have good reasons for saying so. For surely no man in his right mind would set out to make the world the way it is today. Who would deliberately plan all the hate, the sorrow, and the heartbreak which goes to make up our daily headlines? Surely not

God! Surely not man! — at least not man as we would like to imagine him! Who would *deliberately* set man against man, husband against wife, son against father, management against labor, labor against management, nation against nation? Who would *deliberately* make the world the madhouse it is today?

Someone has said facetiously that there is nothing wrong with the world — it's only the people who live in it. Facetious or not, there is a tragic truth which lies behind those words. The only thing wrong with the world today is *people*. At the beginning of the present decade a group of America's greatest scientists called some of the country's leading theologians together and told them in essence:

"Gentlemen, we're frankly frightened. In finally achieving nuclear fission, we've discovered something that will either greatly bless our culture or thoroughly blast it. The threat is not in the explosive power of the atom. We can control that. What we cannot control is the explosive power of human nature. In God's name — if you still believe in God — tell us what you can do to help. Otherwise we perish!"

There is nothing wrong with the atom. There is something wrong with men — all men, common and un-common. The whole of human history and the entire body of human experience stand behind that verdict. Man himself is the worm in the apple! Ignorant or enlightened, illiterate or cultured, behind an ox-drawn plow or behind a panel of electronic knobs and switches — man has always been (and unless redeemed by a power higher than his own, will always be) the world's and his own worst enemy.

What's wrong?

## III

## *THE HUMAN PREDICAMENT*

Something depressing about that last chapter? Remember, there's a purpose behind it. At the end of Chapter I we invited you to take a journey with us "down into the valley — from the bottom of which we shall be able to look up and see the Cross of Christ in its only true significance." The truth is, we haven't gone down nearly far enough. Let's continue our descent.

The Cross of Christ will never mean anything to us as long as we merely bewail the plight of man in general. The next step down the steep descent is to see *ourselves* as members of the human race — equally guilty, equally corrupt, equally unable to unshackle ourselves from the powers that drag us downward. It's true, you had no choice in joining the human race; but the fact is, you belong; and the infection which runs through the bloodstream of the race has infected you no less than any other.

The Christian religion has always insisted that, as far as the spiritual plight of man is concerned, there is no difference between the ignorant aborig-

ine, living in his cave or jungle hut, and the be-
spectacled professor, living among the ivied walls
of a quiet university. No difference between the
woman of the street and the cultured white-haired
matron at her desk in the library. No difference
between the murderer awaiting execution at the
state penitentiary and — you.

A difference in degree, perhaps. But not a difference in kind. We are all members of the human
race. And as members of the human race, we all
carry within our heart the same worm which spreads
the same corruption. The human heart, according
to the Bible, festers with "evil thoughts, murders,
adulteries, fornications, thefts, false witness, blas-
phemies." [1] Not only *some* human hearts, but *all*
human hearts, including yours.

Honesty is not a natural human virtue, but if
we can be only partly honest with ourselves for
even just a moment, we shall have to agree that
what was true of the Apostle Paul is also true of us.
He said once that his own behavior was to him
a source of constant dismay and exasperation, that
he very seldom did the good things he resolved to
do, and that, as sure as death, he would always do
the evil thing he had sworn he would *not* do. He
said there was, as it were, an inexorable principle
operating in his life which dragged him back to

[1] *Matthew 15:19.*

his sin like a dog to his vomit. Nor did he view this situation with indifference or detachment. "It is an agonizing situation," he exclaimed. "Who on earth can set me free from the clutches of my own sinful nature?"[2]

The man who wrote those words was not a drunken sot, not an incorrigible criminal, not a fourth termer, not a candidate for Alcatraz. He was one of the most moral men of his day, the man who did perhaps more than any other human for the spread of the Christian religion. Even in his adult years this noble man had to admit that he was still doing the ugly things he hated and was not doing the beautiful things he knew he should. And what is more, he knew why. As he said, he was in "the clutches of his own sinful nature."

The same nature which holds you in its clutches! How often, after a hundred and one resolutions not to do a certain wicked thing, have you found yourself going ahead and doing it? You were going to quit gossiping, *but you didn't!* You were going to quit being hateful, bitter, cantankerous, uncharitable, suspicious, greedy, selfish, lustful, smutty, jealous, *but you didn't!* You were going to start being kind, loving, gentle, helpful, generous, understanding, pure, clean, and decent, *but you didn't!* You were going to "love the Lord, thy God, with

[2] *Romans 7:14-24. P.*

all thy heart and with all thy soul and with all thy mind," and you were going to "love thy neighbor as thyself," *but you didn't!*

You found again and again that whenever you wanted to say yes to something good, there was a fiendish imp within you that said no; and whenever you wanted to say no to something bad, there was another imp within you that said yes. And more frequently than you like to admit, the noes had it when the yeses should have; and the yeses had it when the noes should have. More frequently than you like to admit, your own behavior baffled you, for you found yourself doing the very things you had promised yourself you wouldn't.

Now, all of this wouldn't be so serious if you had been born a dog or a cat. The fact remains, you were born a human. And God has laid down some very specific laws which govern the relationship between Him and every member of the human family. A cat can scratch a dog and, as far as we know, have no moral responsibility. But no human can scratch another — with a sharp tongue or cutting word — without becoming involved with God. To every human, God has said "Thou shalt" and "Thou shalt not," and any deviation from God's will involves us instantly with Him.

Or do you doubt it? Can you imagine a cat losing its mind because of a guilty conscience —

overcome by a sense of guilt because it swallowed the neighbor's canary? Of course not! Because the cat is not living in a relationship of moral accountability to God. But you are. And because you are, everything you do is subject either to His approval or disapproval. If you were to steal your neighbor's canary, you would immediately hear God's voice of disapproval. Call it conscience or what you will, you know that stealing is contrary to God's will and, for the life of you, you wouldn't want to look God in the face with your neighbor's canary in your hand.

Nor would you want to look God in the face during those moments when you are hateful, angry, selfish, proud. Somehow you know that your perverseness could never stand in the presence of His holiness. Somehow you know that if He is just, He must not only take knowledge of your meanness but, in His justice, He must take action. When sinful Simon Peter found himself in the presence of the sinless Christ, he exclaimed: "Depart from me, for I am a sinful man, O Lord!" [3] And when the Apostle Paul caught the full implication of his own perverseness, he lamented: "It is an agonizing situation. Who on earth can set me free from the clutches of my own sinful nature?" [4]

[3] *Luke 5:8.*  [4] *Romans 7:24. P.*

Like persons who have been told that they are victims of a dread disease, both of these great men were thrown into an "agony" by the frightening realization that the poison of sin which had infected the entire human race had gotten hold of them. They had known it long before, of course, but during those clear moments when they saw their *sinfulness* thrust boldly into the presence of God's *holiness*, they quailed and quaked and quavered. For sinfulness cannot stand in the terrifying presence of holiness.

Paul knew, as you and I should know, that not only the human race in general, but also he in particular was in need of a redemption far above his power to achieve. He knew, as you and I should know, that if he was to be rescued from his own perverseness and restored to divine favor, God would have to do the rescuing.

Paul could not save himself. He was caught, as he ruefully admitted, "in the clutches of his sinful nature," from which, unless he got outside help, there was no escape. And in this, he knew that he was no exception. As he looked out over the mass of sinful humanity and then looked back into his own heart, he said: "There is no difference, for *all* have sinned!" [5]

That is the human predicament!

[5] *Romans 3:22.*

## IV

## OCCUPIED TERRITORY

A dismal picture — those last two chapters? Yes indeed. And in the following pages the picture is going to get even worse. But, once again, let's remember where we're going. We're taking a mental journey downward — down to the bottom of the valley of disillusionment, shedding any illusions which we might have had about the intrinsic moral goodness of the human family.

Our ultimate purpose in this mental journey is not to reach the bottom of the valley but, having reached it, to look up and see the only vision that can make a change in the desperately sordid picture which confronts us. In a sense, the Cross of Christ must forever remain meaningless to the man or woman who views it horizontally. It just *has* to be viewed from a point of vantage which is far below it — and it is toward that point that we are heading.

The Christian religion, as we have pointed out, looks upon every man as being, in the paraphrased words of Paul, "in the clutches of his sinful nature." [1] Again and again it speaks of man as being under "captivity," or under the "dominion" or in the "slavery" of a foreign power. Nor is it speaking figuratively when it uses these expressions. The Christian religion views man as being under a captivity which is as real as that of a prisoner in iron shackles. It views man as being in subjection to a foreign power which determines and controls his thinking and behavior. The Christian religion does not regard natural man, that is, man as he is by birth, as free. In terms that are unmistakable it speaks of man as being born in *bondage*.

When Hitler's hordes invaded Denmark and Norway during the early years of the Great War, they took over completely. The constituted authorities were stripped of their powers, and the citizens were regimented to fit into the Nazi pattern. The will of the occupying power became the law of the land. Freedom of choice, freedom of movement, as well as all those smaller freedoms which we have come to associate with human dignity, were abrogated overnight. The citizens of the occupied countries were free only to carry out the over-all design of the occupying power.

[1] *Romans 7:23. P.*

The analogy may be weak, but we shall make it nevertheless. The human heart has been "occupied territory" ever since that great invasion at the dawn of history when the power of darkness persuaded our first parents to rebel against their Maker. Ever since that day the heart of man, which had been created to be the citadel of God, has been the throne of an alien authority. Man, as we intimated already on a previous page, is indeed "*possessed*" — possessed by an evil power which is bent on his destruction.

That is the starkest and most tragic fact of human history. That is the cataclysmic catastrophe which has cast its blight on humankind. A race possessed, enthralled, in helpless subjugation! A race subjected to a power it cannot see, a power with which it cannot cope. A race which, for all of its enlightenment, is wading through its blood and tears on the road to its own destruction — even though, as it says, it "knows better."

A possessed man may "know better," but as long as he's possessed, he'll do the will of the power that possesses him. And that is the plight of man today. He speaks about love, but he hates. He speaks about truth, but he lies. He speaks about faith, but he is faithless. He speaks about peace, but he causes strife. He speaks about obedience, but he is rebellious. He speaks about moderation, but he goes to excess. He speaks about unselfishness, but he is desperately selfish. He speaks about God in terms of devotion, but he sets himself stubbornly against God and His will. He is hopelessly and helplessly caught in the clutches of a power which is anti-good and anti-God.

(Perhaps we should say briefly here what we are going to say in greater detail later. Namely, that the Bible does not deny to man a certain capacity for morality and decency. The unconverted man can indeed add to or subtract from his moral stature in the eyes of his fellow men. But the Bible does insist that, no matter what his moral stature in the eyes of men, he is still living under an unfriendly spiritual power, which maintains the over-all control. In the eyes of God he is still a member of a race which has turned its back on Him and which, as we shall point out later, is in need of a reconciliation and reinstatement far beyond its own ability to achieve. What the unconverted man needs is not an increase in moral stature but a change in spiritual status.)

Now, what is this mysterious force that has occupied the heart of man and holds him a helpless victim? The Bible speaks of this force under different aspects. The source of all evil, and therefore also of the evil within the human heart, the Bible calls the devil, a personal, powerful, wicked spirit.

The evil principles which the devil has set at work within the human heart the Bible calls by various names. For our present purpose we shall speak of only two of these principles which, as occupying forces within the soul of man, have cast their curse across the whole of humankind. These principles are Sin and Death.

When we say that Sin (arbitrarily spelled with a capital "S") has moved in and taken over the human heart, we are likely to be misunderstood. People today usually think of Sin merely as an isolated moral failure — or as a series of such failures. They think of Sin only as a wrong that has been committed — a wrong from which the perpetrator could have refrained if perhaps he had only counted up to ten. They think of Sin merely as it becomes evident in moral transgression — just as some of us think of a fever merely in terms of a flushed face and forget that somewhere in the body there is an infection which has caused that face to redden.

It is true, individual acts and attitudes *are* sins. Hatred, jealousy, unkindness, these are transgressions of God's Law and are therefore sinful. But when the Bible says that the human race has been "sold under Sin" [2] or has been brought "into captivity to the law of Sin," [3] it is speaking of Sin, not

---

[2] *Romans 7:14.*   [3] *Romans 7:23.*

as a single act, but as a mighty power which holds every member of the human family in its grip.

According to the Christian revelation, Sin is man's master. Sin holds man as its vassal, its slave.[4] While it is correct to say that man has committed sin, it is also correct to say that Sin has committed man — committed him to a life of insurrection and rebellion against his Maker. It is not that man determines whether or not he will sin. It is rather that Sin, that mighty force within, determines that he *shall*. Sin is always and forever in the driver's seat. It would be folly to assume that any man, by a mere act of his will, could get rid of Sin. Sin is his master. He is Sin's captive. And he will continue to do Sin's bidding until Someone who is stronger than Sin steps in to set him free.

Nor is man forced to sin against his will. The insidiousness about this occupation of the human heart is the satanic brainwashing which has rendered every human a willing collaborator with the occupying power. Of the natural man, who is still living under the rule of Sin, the Bible says: "They have their understanding darkened, being alienated from the life of God through the ignorance that is in them, because of the blindness of their heart." [5] Of whom does the Bible say this? Of the human

4 *John 8:34.*        5 *Ephesians 4:18.*

race as it is by nature, that is, as it exists apart from God. In the perverseness of his blinded heart the natural man *wants* to do the bidding of the ugly despot who has taken possession of his soul. His will has been corrupted. He *wants* to do the things he does.

Strange as it may seem, it is difficult to make this horrible truth *real* to many people. Yet all we need do is open our eyes and look at the world in which we live. Is there anything more real in the world than Sin? Has there been any factor in human life more constant — from the dawn of history to this morning's newspaper — than the perverseness of the human heart? Listen for a moment to what Paul wrote to the Romans of his day and see if the shoe doesn't still fit the world in which we live.

"Since they considered themselves too high and mighty to acknowledge God, He allowed them to become the slaves of their degenerate minds, and to perform unmentionable deeds. They became filled with wickedness, rottenness, greed, and malice; their minds became steeped in envy, murder, quarrelsomeness, deceitfulness, and spite. They became whisperers-behind-doors, stabbers-in-the-back, God-haters; they overflowed with insolent pride and boastfulness, and their minds teemed with diabolical invention. They scoffed at duty to parents, they mocked at learning, recognized no obligations of honor, lost all natural affection, and had no use for mercy. More than this — being well aware of God's pronouncement that all who do these things deserve to die, they not only continued their own practices, but made no bones about giving their thorough approval to others who did the same." [6]

That was two thousand years ago. The same description could have been written of each succeeding generation. The heart of natural man has never changed. Who can look at the world today — so confused, so perplexed, so tied in knots, so entangled in the skein of its own iniquity — and still not see the reign of Sin in the heart of man! Murder, strife, bloodshed, envy, greed, selfishness, stubbornness, deceit, dishonesty, adultery, fornication — these are all the henchmen of Sin, the evil power which occupies and rules the human heart.

What power of earth or heaven can drive this merciless invader out?

The other invader and occupier of human life is Death. As in the case of Sin, the Bible looks upon Death not only as a "once in a lifetime" experience which forms the final line in every man's obituary, but as a vicious, monstrous power which holds sway over human life in its totality. The Bible tells us that "by one man Sin entered into the

[6] *Romans 1:28-32. P.*

world, and Death by Sin; and so Death passed upon all men." [7] Our first father, Adam, handed the city key to the invader, who entered in with all his ugly retinue. Since that tragic surrender, Sin and Death have "passed upon all men." Mankind lies helpless in "the bondage of corruption," [8] under the ruthless dominion of Dictator Death.

The Christian religion speaks of Death under three aspects — physical, spiritual, and eternal. What misery, what agony, what paralyzing fear has the specter of physical Death thrown into the heart of man! What rivers of tears have been shed from the dawn of history until this very moment as men, women, and children stood helpless while their loved ones felt the final lash of "the bondage of corruption!" If it were possible, they would have pounded their bleeding fists against heaven's door, pleading for deliverance from the unyielding clutches of this ugly monster.

If ever it was true that "in the midst of life we are in (the midst of) Death," it surely is true today. No other generation in all the history of man has seen as much of Death as ours. Death has literally rained from the skies. Truly, the human race is carrying out the demoniac design of the hellish power which occupies it.

[7] *Romans 5:12.*　　　　[8] *Romans 8:21.*

But physical Death, as we shall point out later, is a terror only to those who are still languishing in the chains of *spiritual* Death. According to the Christian revelation, all of humanity is under the dominion of spiritual Death, a Death far more terrible than that which is merely physical — and far more insidious, since those who are spiritually dead will usually insist that they are spiritually very much alive.

The Apostle Paul, writing to a group of Christian converts in the city of Ephesus, addresses them as "you who were spiritually *dead.*" And then he goes on to tell them that before God had brought them to spiritual life, they had been subject to the "unseen ruler who is still operating in those who do not respond to the truth of God." [9] Until they had been converted to "the truth of God," they were "spiritually dead." They were obeying "the unseen ruler" who had set up his headquarters in their hearts. It will pay you to read the second chapter of Paul's Letter to the Ephesians for a shocking description of man as he is by nature.

Spiritual death was the inevitable lot of a race which turned its back on God, the only Source of Life. Like a leaf severed from its branch, man, after severing himself from God, could be nothing

[9] *Ephesians 2:1, 2. P.*

else but spiritually dead. As a result, the Bible tells us, the natural man cannot lift a finger to improve his spiritual condition. Dead men just don't lift fingers! Natural man, still under the bondage of spiritual Death, cannot loose the shackles which hold him bound. Indeed, he doesn't even see or feel the shackles. He doesn't know that he is bound.

But, worst of all, the final scourge of the dreadful tyrant who holds the race in his relentless grip is Death eternal. "The wages of Sin is Death." [10] The coin of the realm in which the infernal occupying power pays its subjects is — Death forever. The end of natural man, unfreed from the dominion of Sin and Death, is endless separation from his Maker. There will be a life eternal, the Bible tells us, but the man who, when leaving this earth, is still shackled by the powers of Sin and Death shall remain thus shackled into all eternity.

A dreadful thought! A dreadful fact!

We have finally hit the bottom of the valley. Until and unless we are willing to stand right here — in the presence of this dreadful fact — we are not ready to look up to the mountaintop to see the Cross.

[10] *Romans 6:23.*

# V

## A MIGHTY DELIVERANCE

One of the happiest days in the history of little Denmark and Norway and of the other countries which had been invaded and occupied by Hitler's armies was that day in the spring of 1945 when the electrifying message came over the air: "Allied Armies Victorious."

With that victory their long and heavy years of occupation were over. Once again they were free from the grievous yoke of bondage, free from the hand of tyranny, free to live their lives as free men — ransomed from the cruel power of the oppressor.

The decisive battle had not been fought in their own country. Nor had it been fought by their own armies. It had been fought in a different land, and it had been won by the blood and sweat and death of men they had never seen. But they knew that that victory meant their release, for their overpowering enemy had at last gone down in defeat and had been shorn of the power with which he had held them captive.

The analogy which we are about to make is, admittedly, inadequate. But some truths can be grasped more readily by the use of comparison, inadequate though the comparison may be. The Christian message is essentially a message of victory — a victory over those powers of evil which, ever since the surrender of our first parents, have held humanity captive. It is a message of defeat for Sin and Death and a message of triumph for man — a triumph won by a Champion who did battle for the entire human race, on a battlefield two thousand years away.

Christianity, in its simplest terms, is the message of man's deliverance from the horrible occupation of the powers of darkness — by the death and resurrection of God's Son. In that death, as we shall see presently, God Himself paid the ransom which won man's freedom from all his spiritual enemies.

According to the simple words of the Bible, God Himself came down to earth in the person of Jesus Christ. And He had a specific reason for coming — "that through *death* He might destroy him that had the power of death, that is, the devil;

and deliver them who through fear of death were all their lifetime subject to bondage." [1] Again and again the Bible presents the death of Christ as that great act of God by which He set the human race *free* — free not only from the guilt and punishment of Sin, but also from its dreaded power. Or, as Paul puts it, "free from the law of Sin and Death." [2]

That many people have not caught the full force and implication of this message is evidenced by the listless manner in which they hear it. Can you imagine a faithful member of the Norwegian underground greeting the news of the Allied victory on that exciting morning with an indifferent: "How interesting"? For him that message meant the end of an old way of life, a life of fear and dread. It meant a complete change in all of his relationships — to his wife, to his children, to society, to the entire human family. It meant a new day, a new era, a new life, a new world. From the moment he heard the news he began to breathe differently. He had heard a thrilling message, based upon a thrilling fact, and he could be nothing else but thrilled!

The reason why Christianity does not thrill some people today is: they no longer regard it as a *message*. They regard it merely as "a religion,"

[1] *Hebrews 2:14, 15.*        [2] *Romans 8:2.*

whatever that may mean! But if Christianity were no more than "a religion," as that word is commonly understood today, it would be nothing. It is a message about an objective fact, about something that *happened* — the victory of Christ, as the Substitute and Representative of man, over the powers of Sin and Death. If that victory did not take place, Christianity is a myth. If it did, Christianity is a message. And it must be accepted or rejected on that basis.

It is true, every message has a way of becoming dull by endless repetition. Every message has a way of losing its luster with the passing years. The message "Allied Armies Victorious" written in a history book of 1975 will not have nearly the thrill which that same message had when it came across the air in the spring of 1945. Yet the fact which the message heralded in 1945 will be the same fact as long as history books are written. It will always be the fact of a great deliverance.

So, too, the Christian message "Christ Victorious — Mankind Freed" is always in danger of losing its life and luster by the sheer fact of its endless repetition. Men may find it difficult to get excited over a message which, for more than a thousand years, has been spoken in the stilted language of ornate liturgies and religious rituals. But the message is still true; it is still based upon a fact of history.

Whether or not twentieth-century man will be thrilled by the first-century message "Christ Victorious — Mankind Freed" will depend upon a number of things, but first upon his personal awareness of his *need* for such a message. Not everyone in Norway was thrilled by the news of liberation on that day in 1945. There were those in its mental hospitals on that day who were happily indulging their illusions of grandeur — little Napoleons, strutting up and down their asylum wards, utterly oblivious of the true fate of their homeland under the heel of its oppressor. To them the news of the moment was meaningless, because they were unaware of the true state of their beloved Norway. But to those who were aware of the grievous yoke of occupation and of the desperate need for liberation, the news of victory was the signal for ecstatic joy.

Similarly, twentieth-century man — the common man *and* the un-common — if he will give up his feverish dreams of self-sufficiency and will see himself as he really is — sold under Sin, in the bondage of Death and corruption — will react with spontaneous joy to the revelation of the Christian message: "Christ Victorious — Mankind Freed!" Even twentieth-century man, once he has caught the full sweep of this message, will react with the enthusiasm of the ancient seer who said: "How beautiful upon the mountains are the feet of him that bringeth good tidings, that publisheth peace; that bringeth good tidings of good, that publisheth *salvation;* that saith unto Zion, Thy God reigneth!" [3]

But how was Christ's death a victory? And in what sense did that victory bring about man's freedom? Of this we shall speak presently.

[3] *Isaiah 52:7.*

# VI

## A MIGHTY DELIVERER

We stated on a previous page that the Bible presents the death of Christ upon the cross as that great act of God by which He set the human race *free* — free from the bondage of Sin and Death, and from all those spiritual forces which had conspired to bring about man's doom in time and in eternity.

There is much in the above statement that will baffle the uninitiated reader — much that calls for the light of Christian revelation. To claim that the death of Jesus Christ upon the cross could in any way free mankind from the power and punishment of Sin will seem to be utter nonsense until we have learned, first of all, who Jesus Christ is.

Jesus Christ is the Heart and Center of Christian revelation. Only as we learn to know Him, can we hope to know the meaning and the power of His Cross. But once we have learned to know Him for what he claimed and proved Himself to be, the mysteries of His Cross will begin to unfold before the eyes of our awakening faith. Who, then, is this Jesus?

Jesus Christ is God. He is the Second Person in the Holy Trinity: Father, *Son,* and Holy Spirit. He is either that, or He is nothing. He is either that, or the Bible and twenty centuries of Christian witness are a hoax and a fraud. He is either God, or He is not good, because He Himself "made Himself the Son of God." [1] As God, Christ existed before the world began.[2] As God, Christ together with the Father and the Spirit rolled the sun and the moon and the stars into their places. "All things were made by Him." [3] He existed before all worlds, and He will continue to exist after all worlds have crumbled into dust.

In the unsearchable plan of God it was decreed that at a certain point in time, Christ, His Son, should enter the stream of human history. But not without a purpose. When our first parents transgressed the will of God and became subject to the bondage of Sin and Death, God promised to send His eternally pre-existent Son into the world to break the power of Sin and Death and to restore all men to the sonship they had lost.[4] Again and

---

[1] *John 19:7.*          [2] *John 1:1; 8:58.*          [3] *John 1:3.*
[4] *Genesis 3:15.*

again throughout the centuries which followed, God repeated that promise through the lips of His Prophets. These promises, recorded in the Old Testament, are known as the Messianic prophecies. His Son was coming — coming to rescue, to ransom, to redeem a fallen race. That was the theme of the entire Old Testament revelation. Moses, Isaiah, David, Micah, all wrote about the coming Great Deliverer.

And finally, in the stillness of a Palestinian night some two thousand years ago, that promise was fulfilled. The Son of God, who had existed before the world was brought into being, "was made flesh and dwelt among us, and we beheld His glory, the glory as of the Only-begotten of the Father, full of grace and truth." [5] Clothed in mortal flesh, the eternal Son of God spent some thirty-three years on this earth, living and ministering among men, performing mighty deeds, and preaching sublimest truths.

No one who reads the only available biographies of Jesus Christ, those which we have in the Four Gospels, can deny that all four of His biographers were fully convinced that the Man of whom they wrote was indeed the only-begotten Son of God. And at least two of them were intimate friends of the Man of whom they wrote! It is significant that

[5] *John 1:14.*

the biographer who was closest to Christ throughout His public ministry writes toward the close of
his book: "These things are written that ye might
believe that Jesus is the Christ, the *Son of God,*
and that, believing, ye might have life through His
name." [6] John knew who this Man was — and he
wanted the whole world to know!

Again and again, while Christ walked on earth
in human form, He claimed that He was no mere
man, but that He had been sent from heaven by
His Father to accomplish His and His Father's
eternal purpose, or, as He once put it more specifically, "to give His life a ransom for many." [7] On
one occasion, when the people of His day disputed
His claim to divine Sonship, He told them: "Whither
I go, ye cannot come. . . . Ye are from beneath;
I am from above; ye are of this world; I am not
of this world. I said therefore unto you that . . .
if ye believe not that I am He (the Son of God),
ye shall die in your sins." [8] A man who speaks
like that is either the Son of God — or a conceited
egotist — or a refugee from sanity. He is one or
the other. The witness of twenty centuries attests
that this Man was exactly what He claimed to be —
the Son of God.

On another occasion a large number of Christ's
followers deserted Him. When He turned to His

[6] *John 20:31.*      [7] *Matthew 20:28.*
[8] *John 8:21-24.*

faithful few and asked: "Will ye also go away?"
it was Simon Peter who answered in the name of
them all: "Lord, to whom shall we go? Thou hast
the words of eternal life: And we believe and are
sure that Thou art that Christ, the *Son of the living
God.*" [9] So utterly convinced was Simon Peter that
Jesus Christ was indeed the Son of the living God,
that many years later he himself laid down his own
life rather than deny this fundamental truth of
which he was so sure.

It is not our purpose in these few pages to
marshal all the evidences of the deity of Christ —
His miracles, His sinlessness, and the divine qual-
ities which the Bible ascribes to Him, such qual-
ities, for instance, as omnipotence,[10] omniscience,[11]
and omnipresence.[12] But we shall mention one more
evidence of the type which is most likely to im-
press. There is no greater proof for the deity (God-
ship) of Jesus Christ than His resurrection from the
grave on Easter morning. On more than one occasion Christ had told His friends (also His enemies)
that He would be put to death, but that He would
arise again on the third day.[13] Now, there are few
surer ways of making oneself ridiculous than predict-
ing that one will return from the grave. Others
have made such a promise. The difference between

[9] *John 6:68, 69.*          [10] *Hebrews 1:1-3.*
[11] *John 21:17.*          [12] *Matthew 28:18-20.*
[13] *Matthew 16:21; 27:63; John 2:19.*

them and Christ is that Christ made the promise —
and *kept* it. And that makes all the difference in
the world.

Few facts in history have been more firmly at-
tested than the resurrection of Jesus Christ. Among
the very first to verify the fact of His resurrection
were His enemies.[14] Among the slowest to believe
the almost unbelievable report were His own disciples.[15] But so overwhelming was the evidence that
within a few weeks all of these men who were so
reluctant to believe were proclaiming throughout
the world: "The Lord is risen! The Lord is risen
indeed!"

The story of Christ's resurrection is not a legend
which grew with the years. It was only seven weeks
after it happened that Peter addressed a huge mass
meeting in Jerusalem and boldly declared: "This
Jesus hath God raised up, whereof we all are wit-
nesses." [16] Seven weeks is a short time — not long
enough for legends to grow. Anyone who is willing
to read the record and to take the record at its
word will have no doubt: the Man who was born
in Bethlehem some two thousand years ago, who
performed marvelous deeds and preached profound
truths, who was crucified, who rose again on Easter

14 *Matthew 27:62-66; 28:11-15.*
15 *Matthew 28:17; Mark 16:11; Luke 24:11; John 20:25.*
16 *Acts 2:32.*

morning, and who forty days later ascended visibly into heaven [17] — this Man was in truth the only-begotten Son of God.

This is a pivotal truth. It is important that we pin it down securely if we are to see any connection whatever between the two statements of the opening chapter of this book: "Jesus died," and therefore "our sins are forgiven." As the eternal and sinless Son of God, Jesus Christ was not subject to the bondage of Sin and Death. He did not have to die. And yet He *died!* Why? What was the purpose of His death? What was the meaning of His Cross?

[17] *Acts 1:9-11.*

## VII

## *A DIVINE MYSTERY*

With this chapter we are about to enter the inner room, in which we are brought face to face with the climax mystery of Christian revelation. We use the words "mystery" and "revelation" with good purpose. We say "mystery," because we are fully aware that after we have said all that the Bible has to say on this subject, there will still be many questions left unanswered. There will always be many aspects of the death of Christ and its relationship to human sin which will be nothing more nor less than — *mystery*. But the essentials of this relationship can be made clear to anyone who understands the rules of ordinary language.

We say "revelation," because there is no other way by which the human mind could be informed of the significance of the Cross of Christ than by an act of divine revelation. The Christian religion is not a "natural" religion, not a religion arrived at by the ordinary processes of natural reason. It is a religion of revelation, revealed by God — in Scripture.

No one knew that better than the Apostle Paul, the chief propagator of the Christian message during the first century. After telling the early Christians that he had but one message, namely, "Jesus Christ, and Him Crucified," [1] Paul assured them that this message was not the product of his or any other human mind, but that it was the revelation of God. He said that in proclaiming the death of Christ as the salvation of the world he was preaching "the wisdom of God in a *mystery*." This mystery, he said, was something "which none of the princes of this world knew. . . . But, as it is written, Eye hath not seen, nor ear heard, neither have entered into the heart of man the things which God hath prepared for them that love Him. But God hath *revealed* them unto us by His Spirit." [2] In other words, whatever we know about "Christ, and Him Crucified" — the death of Christ and its relation to human sin, we can learn from only one source: divine revelation, the inspired Bible.

Well, then, what does the Bible tell us?

The writers of the Bible look upon the entire history of the human race as a vast panorama, with the Cross of Christ at its center. What happened *before* the death of Christ was prolog. What hap-

[1] *1 Corinthians 2:2.*          [2] *1 Corinthians 2:7-10.*

pened *after* the death of Christ is epilog. As a great mountain casts its morning shadow to the West and its evening shadow to the East, so the Cross of Christ, standing at the great divide of human history, casts its morning shadow across the centuries that preceded it and continues to cast its evening shadow across all the centuries that follow it. The world has *always* lived in one relation or the other to the Cross of Christ.

Throughout the centuries of the Old Testament the believers looked forward toward the Cross. They looked forward to an act of deliverance which would forever free them from the guilt, the power, and the punishment of sin. They looked forward to a heaven-sent Deliverer who would heal the breach which sin had torn between the Creator and the creature. They looked forward to a great act of atonement, by which God would forever erase the debt of guilt which lay on every human conscience and absolve all men from the hideous consequence of their transgressions.

Where did they get this expectation? From God Himself. By revelation. Through His Prophets God had given His Law to humankind, particularly the Moral Law, as it is summarized in His holy Ten Commandments. But man rebelled against his Maker and refused to obey His laws, with the result that God, in His holiness, pronounced His curse on

the entire human family. Again and again, through
His Prophets, God proclaimed His terrible judgment
upon the sins of men. In His justice and His holiness He could do nothing else. But in His love —
He found a way, a way to extricate sinful man from
his horrible dilemma.

To those who lived on the morning-side of the
Cross (that is, to those who lived in the Old Testament era) He gave an elaborate system of "atonement," whereby the human conscience could be
cleansed from the guilt of its iniquity. This system
of atonement runs throughout the entire Jewish
ritual which God gave to His people through the
Prophet Moses. Large and learned volumes could
be written on the various Old Testament rituals of
atonement, but for our present purpose we shall
limit ourselves to the following simple summary.

At God's direction the believers of the Old
Testament "made payment" for their sin by sym-
bolically transferring their guilt to an animal
(a bullock, a sheep, or a lamb, as prescribed by the
Law) and then sacrificing that animal as a sym-
bolic atonement for their transgressions. This, we
repeat, was done by divine direction.[3] Thus, in
symbol, the sinner transferred his guilt to the innocent, and the innocent died in the place of the
guilty.

[3] *E. g., Leviticus 16:5-10.*

But how could the death of a lamb make good
for the sins of a human being? It couldn't. That
is, not in itself. High on the great divide which
still lay centuries in the future stood that Great
Sacrifice which alone could give meaning and value
to all the rivers of blood which were shed in Jewish
temples. The death of Christ was the *real* thing —
of which the death of the Old Testament lamb was
but a shadow. The death of the sacrificial lamb
had atoning value for the Old Testament believer
only because the Old Testament believer had put
his faith in a greater Lamb, whom God had promised him and who was to make final payment for
all of his transgressions.

Just as a ten-dollar bill has value, not because
of the worth of the paper it is printed on, but
because of secure collateral which may lie a thousand miles away, so the death of the sacrificial lamb
in the Old Testament had atoning value only because of the immeasurable collateral which was still
to be won on the Cross of Calvary. Speaking of
the Old Testament sacrifices, the New Testament
says that these were "a shadow of things to come,
but the body is of Christ." [4]

One day during that eventful period when the
era of the Old Testament was blending into the
New, John the Baptist saw Jesus approaching him

[4] *Colossians 2:17.*

in the region of the River Jordan. For some it was the first time they had met this Man of Nazareth. Pointing to Jesus, John called to those about him and said: "Behold the Lamb of God, which taketh away the sin of the world!" [5] This man John, who had been divinely appointed [6] as the forerunner of the Savior, knew, with an insight which had been given to him by God, that here atop the summit of human history had at last appeared *the* Lamb — the Lamb of *God* — the final and ultimate Sacrifice for the entire heap of human sin.

Did Jesus of Nazareth regard Himself to be that Lamb — the Lamb who had been prefigured throughout all of Old Testament history? On the night before His death He celebrated the Jewish Passover meal with His disciples. This meal had been celebrated by the Jews for fifteen centuries in commemoration of the night when they were delivered from Egyptian bondage. On the night of the first Passover every Jewish family had killed a lamb and had daubed its blood upon the doorposts of its home — a signal for the angel of death to "pass over" their household.

Obedient to Jewish tradition, Christ had just completed His last Passover meal. Tomorrow He would die. Remnants of the roasted lamb and unleavened bread were still on the table. Taking

[5] *John 1:29.*      [6] *Luke 1:13-17.*

some of the fragments of bread, He gave them to His friends and said: "Take, eat, this is MY body which is given for you." Note that "My body" — no longer the body of a lamb. Against the backdrop of the evening's celebration, so replete with symbols, His words were fraught with deepest meaning for His friends. Then, taking the cup, He offered it to them and said: "This is MY blood of the NEW testament, which is shed for many for the remission of sins."[7] Note that "My blood" and the "New testament" — no longer the blood of an Old Testament lamb. Yes, Jesus knew that His great sacrifice was the substance of which all Old Testament sacrifices were but the shadow.[8] He knew, as He had told His intimate friends, that He had come into the world "to give His life a ransom for many."[9]

That His disciples understood the relation of Christ's death to the sacrifices of the Old Testament is clearly evident from their later writings. Paul writes to the Corinthians: "Christ, our Passover, is sacrificed for us."[10] And Peter writes to the scattered believers of the early church: "Ye were . . . redeemed . . . with the precious blood of Christ, as of a Lamb without blemish and without spot."[11] Anyone who was acquainted with the doctrine of

[7] *Luke 22:19.*  [8] *Colossians 2:17.*
[9] *Matthew 20:28.*  [10] *1 Corinthians 5:7.*
[11] *1 Peter 1:18, 19.*

"atonement" as it was embodied in page after page of the Jewish ritual knew what Paul and Peter meant by such references.

To the orthodox Jew of Paul's day, acquainted as he was with his rituals of atonement, there could be no mistaking the meaning of the New Testament message: "Christ, Our Passover, is sacrificed for us." He may not have agreed with the message, but he would have had no trouble understanding the language. The tragedy of our day is that the common man has so little knowledge of the Old Testament — and therefore has no backdrop against which to silhouette the Cross.

Of the two Testaments of the Bible someone has said:

> The New is in the Old contained,
> The Old is in the New explained;
> The New is in the Old concealed,
> The Old is in the New revealed.

No one who is acquainted with both Testaments of the Bible and who is willing to take them *as they read* — without the admixture of preconceived notions or opinions — will doubt that Jesus Christ is the Lamb of God and that, as the Lamb of God, He died to bear the sins of all mankind.

That both Christ and His followers and the early Christian church were clearly and fully agreed on the atoning significance of His death, we shall see in the following.

## VIII

## *PAID IN FULL*

Most men want to be remembered because of their life — because of something they did or said. It is significant, however, that Jesus, the Man who died at the youthful age of 33, wanted to be remembered chiefly because of His death. On more than one occasion He took His disciples into His confidence and told them about His coming death by crucifixion.

He pointed to His crucifixion, which in His divine foreknowledge He clearly foresaw, as the culmination of His purpose here on earth. As important as was His life, He knew that in the over-all accomplishment of His purpose His *death* would be even more important. To His disciples He said: "And I, if I be lifted up from the earth [on the cross], will draw all men unto Me." [1] And to Nicodemus, who had come to Him by night, He said:

[1] *John 12:32.*

"And as Moses lifted up the serpent in the wilderness, even so must the Son of Man be lifted up [on a cross], that whosoever believeth in Him should not perish, but have eternal life." [2]

That it was His death, more than His life, that He wanted His followers to remember was clear also from His institution of the Lord's Supper and His command: "This do in remembrance of Me." [3] This particular significance of the Lord's Supper was later echoed by Paul when he wrote to the early Christians: "As often as ye eat this bread and drink this cup, ye do show the Lord's *death* till He come." [4] Or as J. B. Phillips paraphrases this verse: "Whenever you eat this bread or drink of this cup, you are proclaiming that the Lord has died for you, and you will do that until He comes again."

The earliest Christian literature shows that it was the *death* of Christ — much more than His wonderful sermons and mighty miracles — that occupied the chief attention of the early church. When the first missionaries went out (only a matter of weeks after Christ's resurrection) it was the death of Christ that formed the heart and center of their message. Paul summarized his entire missionary message thus: "I declare unto you the Gospel which I preached unto you . . . how that Christ *died* for

[2] *John 3:14, 15.*        [3] *Luke 22:19.*
[4] *1 Corinthians 11:26.*

our sins according to the Scriptures and that He was buried and that He rose again the third day according to the Scriptures." [5] Paul was referring here, of course, to the Old Testament Scriptures. The fact that Christ *died* was the cornerstone upon which Paul's whole message was built. As he himself said, he was determined to know only one thing: "Christ, and Him Crucified." [6]

As the message of early Christianity spread throughout Palestine and Asia Minor, to Northern Africa, to Greece and Rome, the Cross inevitably became the symbol of the Christian Gospel. Evidently there was something about the Cross of Christ, His death by crucifixion, which made it of supreme significance in the theology of the early Christians. What was that significance?

The New Testament puts it very plainly. Here are a few representative statements: "Christ died for our sins." [7] "We were reconciled to God by the death of His Son . . . by whom we have now received the *atonement*." [8] "He His own self bare our sins in His own body on the tree." [9] "Christ hath redeemed us from the curse of the Law, being made a curse for us." [10] "God commendeth His love toward us in that, while we were yet sinners, Christ

---

[5] *1 Corinthians 15:1-4.*   [6] *1 Corinthians 2:2.*
[7] *1 Corinthians 15:3.*   [8] *Romans 5:10, 11.*
[9] *1 Peter 2:24.*   [10] *Galatians 3:13.*

died for us." [11]  "In Him we have redemption through His blood, the forgiveness of sins." [12]  "God made Him to be sin for us who knew no sin." [13] Or that classic study in pronouns given us by the Old Testament Prophet Isaiah: "Surely, He hath borne our griefs and carried our sorrows. . . . He was wounded for our transgressions, He was bruised for our iniquities. The chastisement of our peace was upon Him, and with His stripes we are healed. . . . The Lord hath laid upon *Him* the iniquity of *us* all." [14]

This, then, is the significance of the death of Christ, according to the Bible: as the sins of men in the Old Testament were transferred to the lamb *in symbol* and were atoned for by its death in the sinners' stead, so the guilt of all mankind has been transferred to Jesus Christ, the Lamb of God, *in fact,* and has been atoned for by His substitutionary death upon the cross.

Christ died. He died for us. He died for our sins. He died to pay the entire debt of human guilt. And in His unsearchable love and wisdom God in heaven has agreed to accept *Christ's* payment as the settlement of *our* account. That is the "new agreement," the "new covenant," the "new testament in Christ's blood." [15]  Christ, as it were, has picked up

---

[11] *Romans 5:8.*          [12] *Ephesians 1:7.*
[13] *2 Corinthians 5:21.*          [14] *Isaiah 53:4-6.*
[15] *Matthew 26:28.*

all of the moral I. O. U.'s of the human race, all of the accumulated moral debts of every member of the human family which were owed to God and has "blotted them out," has "taken them out of the way," has "nailed them to His Cross." [16] Or, as Paul once put it: "God was in Christ, reconciling the world unto Himself, not imputing [charging] their trespasses unto them, and hath committed unto us the Word of Reconciliation." [17]

Now, we realize of course this may all sound quite fanciful to some. It may be all right for a man to say that he came into the world to "give his life a ransom" [18] and to say that, because of his substitutionary death, God has entered into a "new agreement" with the human race whereby He is willing to cancel all accounts. It may be all right for his friends to talk about God's being willing to wipe the slate clean because of the substitutionary payment of His Son. [19] The question is: *Does God agree?* Is this "new agreement," this "new testament," bona fide? Does it have substance? Does it have value? Does it have any Word of God behind it? Or is it merely the pious dream of wishful and misguided men?

All of these questions were answered for all men and for all time on the first Easter morning. Christ

[16] *Colossians 2:14.*     [17] *2 Corinthians 5:19.*
[18] *Matthew 20:28.*      [19] *Romans 3:19-28; 1 John 1:7.*

not only *died* for the sin of men; He *rose* again!
Had Christ remained in the grave, all talk of His
having paid the debt of human sin would be idle.
As the Bible puts it, "if Christ be not raised, your
faith is vain; ye are yet in your sins; then they also
which are fallen asleep in Christ [those who have
died trusting in Him] are perished." [20]

The Bible gives the Easter resurrection a stra-
tegic role in God's great drama of redemption.[21]
Without the Easter message, proclaimed as a certain and historical fact, there could be no Christian
Gospel. Not only does Christ's resurrection demonstrate, beyond all doubt, that He was, and *is*, the
eternal Son of God and that therefore all of His
doctrines must be true; but it also demonstrates,
beyond all shadow of doubt, that God in heaven
has accepted the sacrifice of His Son for the sins
of all the world.

The Easter miracle is heaven's receipt, presented
to all men of all ages, saying: "Payment Received —
Paid in Full!" When God the Father raised His
Son from the grave, He was saying in effect to every
member of the human race: "I have accepted the
ransom which My Son has brought in payment for
your sin. His resurrection is the stamp and seal of
My divine approval. His resurrection is not only

[20] *1 Corinthians 15:17, 18.*
[21] *Romans 1:4; 4:25; 1 Corinthians 15:51-57.*

*His* vindication — but also yours. For, because of His payment which I have now accepted in your stead, you are free!" Indeed, that is what the Scriptures say when they tell us: "Christ was delivered for our offenses and raised again for our justification." [22] He went into death because of our transgressions, and He was raised from the dead to demonstrate that, in the sight of His Father, our transgressions had indeed been atoned. He who grasps the significance of the Easter miracle can have no doubt that "God *was* in Christ, reconciling the world unto Himself, not imputing [charging] their trespasses unto them." [23]

(Let us pause, parenthetically, to observe that we have been speaking of Christ largely in the past tense. That was inevitable since we were speaking of His Cross as an event in human history. However, once we have grasped the full significance of Jesus Christ and His Cross, we shall begin to speak of Him in the *present*. Jesus Christ is not dead! He is the "ever-living," [24] "ever-present," [25] "ever-reigning," [26] Lord of heaven and earth. He is living and reigning right now, not only over the material universe, which He rules with His divine power, but also, and especially, over the hearts of His

[22] *Romans 4:25.*      [23] *2 Corinthians 5:19.*
[24] *Hebrews 7:25.*      [25] *Matthew 28:20.*
[26] *Revelation 1:6.*

redeemed, over whom He rules with His divine grace.) [27]

But to revert to the main stream of our chapter: the message of the early Christian Church and, for that matter, the message of the church at all times, wherever it has remained true to its trust, was and always will be simply and wonderfully this: Jesus Christ, the Son of God, died in the place of human-kind in order that He might pay for the sum total of human sin. And by means of the resurrection miracle on Easter morning God the Father proclaimed to all the world that He has accepted the payment of His Son.

Because of the sacrifice of the Son, which has been accepted by the Father in payment for the world's iniquity, humanity has been forgiven. And, forgiven, it is free! [28]

[27] *Matthew 28:18; Colossians 1:13 20.*
[28] *John 8:34-36*

## IX

## *THE LAW FULFILLED*

It would be a mistake to restrict our conception of "the Cross of Christ" to those six hours during which He hung suspended on that instrument of torture. While it is true that His death was the supreme act of atonement for human guilt, it is also true that His entire life was a part of God's great plan of reconciliation. In a sense, there was never a moment, between His conception in His virgin mother and His final dying gasp upon the cross, when He was *not* suffering and serving as the great Substitute of humankind.

To make this point clear, let us look once more at the great human predicament of which we spoke in our earlier chapters. God had given His Law to man. Not only had He written His Law within the human heart, but through Moses He had given it in the form of the Ten Commandments. And He had made it clear that, in His holiness, He could

57

brook no disobedience. Transgression would inevitably mean punishment. If God were to remain God, His Law would have to be kept.

But man rebelled. Man transgressed. And in his fallen state, possessed as he was by the powers of Sin and Death, he was hopelessly unable to meet the stern requirements of a Law which demanded moral perfection. As long as that Law stood unfulfilled, there was an unbridgeable chasm between the just and holy God on the one hand and sinful man on the other. No human being could step into the presence of the Divine, except on those terms which had been laid down by the Divine; and since those terms demanded perfect conformity with the laws of God, the separation between God and man was complete and hopeless. If the chasm was ever to be bridged, it would have to be bridged from God's side.

Since God is not only holy but also merciful, He bridged that chasm Himself. He decided to keep His own Law — and to keep it in the place and for the benefit of sinful men who couldn't!

It is right here that Christianity differs from all so-called "world religions." According to the Christian revelation, God is not only holy, but He is also merciful. And in His mercy He decided to *act* in man's behalf. In His unsearchable wisdom He decided to step into the stream of human history and, blending divine justice with divine mercy, work out a plan which would bridge the gap between Him and His fallen children. He decided to keep His own Law — and to keep it in the place of spiritually helpless men!

The Bible tells us that "when the fullness of the time was come, God sent forth His Son, made of a woman, made *under* the Law, to redeem them that were under the Law, that we might receive the adoption of sons."[1] Similarly, the Bible tells us in another place — and we shall paraphrase the passage, since the language of the Bible in our English translations is somewhat difficult: "Christ, who had always been God by nature, did not insist on His divine prerogatives, but consented to become a servant and to be born a mortal man. And having become a man, He humbled Himself by living a life of complete obedience."[2] God obedient! Obedient to what? To the Law which He Himself had given!

In other words, He who was above the Law willingly put Himself beneath it. He who had given the Commandment chose to address the Commandment to Himself — and fulfill it. And He chose to do this as the divine Substitute for those who, because of their spiritual bondage, were unable to do it for themselves. His life of moral perfection

---

[1] *Galatians 4:4, 5.*     [2] *Philippians 2:6-8.*

which He lived throughout His visit here on earth
was lived not for Himself, but as a part of that
great "agreement" (testament) whereby God volun-
teered to do everything that was necessary to bring
about a perfect reconciliation between Himself and
hopeless man.

This aspect of Christ's redeeming work, we know,
is little mentioned today. But His redeeming *life*
is taught in Scripture just as clearly as His redeeming *death*. In the fifth chapter of his Letter to the
Romans, Paul draws a striking analogy. He says
that just as the sin of Adam resulted in the spiritual
enslavement of all mankind, so the righteousness
of Christ (written to the credit of all generations
of the human family) has resulted in their emanci-
pation — and in their acceptance before the bar of
Heaven's justice. This is how Paul puts it: "We
see, then, that as one act of sin [Adam's] exposed
the whole race of men to God's judgment and
condemnation, so one act of perfect righteousness
[Christ's] presents all men freely acquitted in the
sight of God. One man's disobedience placed all
men under the threat of condemnation, but one
Man's obedience has the power to present all men
righteous before God." [3]

Admittedly, we are here dealing with an aspect
of Christian revelation which Paul himself would

[3] *Romans 5:18, 19. P.*

list on his heavier diet — of spiritual "meat, not milk." [4] Yet it should not be too difficult to grasp, once we have learned to look upon Christ — in all that He did and suffered — as the great *Representative* of humankind. Nothing that He did, while here on earth, was really done for Himself. As the eternal, ever-living, ever-reigning Son of God, He did not have to be born, He did not have to assume human flesh, He did not have to keep the Law, He did not have to suffer and die. Whatever He did He did vicariously — that is, as a Substitute, for someone else, for the benefit of others. For us. For you. And this vicarious nature attached also to His keeping of the Law, to His perfect righteousness. Just as His suffering was for us — for our benefit — so also was His righteousness. He kept God's law — for us!

That the Apostle Paul caught the full force of this theological truth and applied it to his own life is evident from a remark which he makes in one of his Letters. He says to the Philippians: "Not having mine *own righteousness,* which is of the Law, but that which is through the faith of Christ, the righteousness which is of God by faith." [5] We do not want to anticipate here what we shall say later, but it is evident that Paul looked upon the perfect righteousness of Christ as something which,

---

[4] *1 Corinthians 3:2.*　　　　　[5] *Philippians 3:9.*

in some manner, had become his, Paul's. He was confident that, even though he had no righteousness of his own, he would be able to stand before God on Judgment Day in the righteousness of Christ. Somehow that righteousness would avail for *him*.

Christ was Paul's Representative before God, then, not only when He died but also when He lived — when He lived in submission to a Law which He did not have to keep but which He kept, nevertheless, because He knew Paul couldn't.

That, too, was part of "the Cross."

## X

## A SPOKESMAN IN HEAVEN

In a sense it is unfortunate that in any treatment of the Cross of Christ and its significance to contemporary man we are forced to use verbs which are preponderantly in the past tense. Yet, as we have pointed out, this is inevitable, since the Cross is an event in history, an event which transpired nearly 2,000 years ago. No one can write or speak of that event without using verbs whose tense is in the past. Yet in a very real and important sense, the Cross of Christ is an ever-present, ever-powerful fact today, tomorrow, and forever. If it is true that Christ is the eternal Contemporary, it is also true that His Cross has a significance and a power which are available to men of every age.

The early Christians, as they spread their Gospel throughout the Greek and Roman world, spoke of their Savior not as a dead man who had accomplished his purpose in life and had left them to carry on where he left off. They spoke of Him rather as one who was very much alive, still active in behalf of those for whom He died. Christ had been crucified, it is true, and by His death He had won a limitless reservoir of spiritual blessings for all mankind; but that was not where His activity in behalf of sinful man had ended. He was still alive in His Father's house above, still active in behalf of His brethren, still dispensing and distributing those spiritual gifts which, by His Cross, He had won for man.

This is a major point, especially of the Epistle to the Hebrews. These Christian Jews were told that "Christ is able to save them to the uttermost that come unto God by Him, seeing He *ever liveth* to make intercession for them." [1] He was still alive, still abundantly able to save anyone who would come to God through Him. Just as the ancient Jewish priest was ordained, by God's command, to make intercession for the people, that is, to serve as a go-between between God and man, so Christ, the eternal High Priest, was ordained to be the eternal Intercessor. The New Testament writers make very much of this continuing intercession of the Savior before the throne of His Father. The Hebrew Christians are told that Christ has gone "into heaven itself, now to appear in the presence of God *for us*." [2] John writes to his followers: "If

---

[1] *Hebrews 7:25.*     [2] *Hebrews 9:24.*

any man sin, we have an Advocate [one who speaks for us] with the Father, Jesus Christ, the Righteous; and He is the Propitiation [the payment] for our sins, and not for ours only, but also for the sins of the whole world." [3] And Paul speaks to the Romans about "Christ that died, yea, rather, that is risen again, who is even at the right hand of God, who also maketh intercession for us." [4] Clearly, the Bible speaks of the resurrected and ascended Christ as the *interceding* Christ, as humanity's Intercessor before His Father's throne.

Admittedly, there is much about this aspect of Christian revelation which goes beyond the ability of the finite mind to grasp. Perhaps chief among the reasons for this is the inability of the human mind to mesh time into eternity. If Christ won a complete redemption, a complete reconciliation, for us by the historical acts of His birth, life, death, and resurrection 1900 years ago, why must He keep on interceding for us with His heavenly Father? From the human point of view this would seem to be unnecessary. Nevertheless, for the comfort of believers of every age the Bible *does* present Christ as the ever-living Intercessor before the throne of heaven. This the believer accepts in faith. Whether a man lived in the first century, the fifteenth, or the twentieth, the Bible assures him

[3] *1 John 2:1.*     [4] *Romans 8:34.*

that Christ is his Contemporary — that Christ is his contemporary Spokesman with the Father.

In the court of heaven Christ is forever pleading the merits of His Cross as the ransom for the sinner. As if He were to say: "I know, heavenly Father, that Bill Jones transgressed Your Commandments and is worthy to be cast forever from Your sight. But it was for Bill Jones that I went down to earth to keep the Commandments. It was for him and his transgressions that I paid the penalty when I died upon the cross. My Cross was for him. And so, heavenly Father, Bill Jones's account is settled. He *must* go free. That is Our agreement. Our covenant. Our Testament."

The above may be what theologians call an anthropomorphism (speaking of God as though He were a man), but in reality it says nothing more than the Apostle John said when he wrote to the early Christians (and we shall paraphrase his words into our idiom): "Whenever any one of us falls into sin, let's remember, we have a Spokesman with the Father in heaven, Someone who will put in a good word for us. And He is Jesus Christ, the Righteous One, who kept the Law for us and who by His death rendered complete satisfaction for all our sins, and not for our sins only but for the sins of the entire human race." [5]

[5] *1 John 2:1.*

No one who reads the record can deny that to the early Christians Jesus Christ was humanity's Advocate before the bar of heaven's justice. And, as the writer of the Letter to the Hebrews points out, Jesus Christ is "the same yesterday, today, and forever." [6] What He was to the Christian in Rome or Corinth or Ephesus, He is still to the Christian in New York, Chicago, or Los Angeles.

We cannot conclude this discussion of the intercessory work of Christ without at least a passing word on its relation to the practice of Christian prayer. There can be no Christian prayer without an understanding of the Cross. And, conversely, an understanding of the Cross makes Christian prayer one of the simplest exercises of the Christian faith.

Christ told His disciples to approach His Father in His (Christ's) name. "Verily, verily, I say unto you, Whatsoever ye shall ask the Father *in My name*, He will give it you." [7] Now, what did He mean by that? Perhaps we can best approximate the meaning of the Savior's thought by a simple illustration. A distinguished gentleman, walking down the street of a large city, once happened upon a ragged beggar whom he recognized as one of his boyhood schoolmates. After exchanging a few remarks with the man, he drew a piece of paper from his pocket and wrote a few words on it.

[6] *Hebrews 13:8.*    [7] *John 16:23.*

Handing the slip of paper to his ragged friend, he suggested that he take it to a certain men's furnishing store, where he would be fitted out with a new suit of clothing. "But how do I know I won't be thrown out of the store?" the unfortunate man protested. "After all, I don't have more than a nickel to my name." The distinguished gentleman replied with a reassuring smile: "You won't need your nickel. All you need is my name. And I've written it as plain as day at the bottom of that slip of paper." Within an hour the ragged man was wearing a brand-new outfit. He had acted on his friend's suggestion and had found that the name of his friend was good. It was indeed all he needed.

Ragged humanity has no more right to step into the holy presence of God with its petitions than that beggar, acting on his own, had a right to step into that clothing shop and ask for a suit of clothes. Of the entire human race the Bible says: "We are all as an unclean thing, and all our righteousnesses are as filthy rags." [8] Natural man, besmeared and besmirched by sin as he is, has no credit in heaven upon which he can draw. The only credit that will avail is the credit of the Cross, that great act of atonement which has won forgiveness for human sin and has put God and man on speaking terms.

[8] *Isaiah 64:6.*

It was Christ, the sin-atoning Savior, who said: "I am the Way, the Truth, and the Life; no man cometh to the Father but by Me." [9]

The only credit the beggar had was his friend's name. And the only credit you and I have that will entitle us to approach God in prayer is the name of Christ. "Whatsoever ye shall ask the Father in My name." And His name will avail because His Cross has made us acceptable to the Father. A Christian poet once put down in beautiful and exalted language what it means to pray to God in the name of Christ. He wrote:

> I do not come because my soul
> Is free from sin and pure and whole
> And worthy of Thy grace;
> I do not speak to Thee because
> I've ever justly kept Thy laws,
> And dare to meet Thy face.
>
> I know that sin and guilt combine
> To reign o'er every thought of mine
> And turn from good to ill;
> I know that when I try to be
> Upright and just and true to Thee,
> I am a sinner still.
>
> I know that, though in doing good
> I spend my life, I never could
> Atone for all I've done;
> But though my sins are black as night,
> I dare to come before Thy sight
> Because I trust Thy Son.

[9] *John 14:6.*

In *Him alone* my trust I place —
Come boldly to Thy throne of grace,
    And there commune with Thee.
Salvation sure, O Lord, is mine,
And, all unworthy, I am Thine,
    For Jesus died for me!

That, and nothing less, is praying in the name of Christ. Notice the climactic nature of the poet's very last line. Why does he make bold to approach the throne of God with his petitions? Where does he get his confidence? Whence the assurance that his petitions will be heard? Whence the intimate fellowship which enables him to speak to God "as a dear son to his dear father"? Not because of any right or merit of his own! Not because of any credit of *his* which entitles him to an audience with the God of heaven! No, his confidence and assurance come only from the Cross.

And, all unworthy, I am Thine,
For Jesus died for me!

And this Jesus, who died for him in time, has been ordained by God to be his Spokesman in all eternity.

## XI

## *THE WAY OF FAITH*

To the reader who has stayed with us thus far, it has doubtless become evident that we have made some startling statements — statements which he perhaps never dreamed were an essential part of the Christian message. Yet, in the main, we have said nothing to which every Bible-believing church in the world today would not subscribe. What, really, have we said thus far? Simply this: that man, by nature, is alienated from God as a result of sin; that, left to his own devices, he would remain forever lost; but that Christ, the eternal Son of God, has wrought a mighty deliverance through His substitutionary death upon the cross. That is, in outline, what we have said thus far, and that is, substantially, what all Christians believe.

But now the question! If Christ by His redeeming death upon the cross has won complete salvation for all mankind, then why is it that some people continue to be lost? If God in heaven has proclaimed a universal amnesty because of the sacrificial life and death of His beloved Son in the place of all mankind, then why is it that much of mankind continues under the thraldom of the despots Sin and Death? If Christ has opened the doors of heaven with the lever of His Cross, then why do people continue to go to hell?

A learned man visited the Savior one night. They discussed knotty theological problems until the wee hours of the morning. Among the things that Jesus said that night we find at least part of the answer to the question we have posed. Speaking to Nicodemus, a leader of the Jews, Jesus said: "And as Moses lifted up the serpent in the wilderness, even so must the Son of Man be lifted up, that whosoever believeth in Him should not perish, but have eternal life. For God so loved the world that He gave His only-begotten Son, that whosoever believeth in Him should not perish, but have everlasting life. For God sent not His Son into the world to condemn the world, but that the world through Him might be saved. He that believeth on Him is not condemned; but he that believeth not is condemned already, because he hath not believed in the name of the only-begotten Son of God. And this is the condemnation, that light is come into the world and men loved darkness rather than light." [1]

[1] *John 3:14-19.*

From these words of Jesus, and from many other statements in the Bible, it is clear that God has established *a way* by which the individual human being is to lay hold of the blessings of the Cross. That way is faith! Redemption has been secured for all mankind — redemption, full, free, and final — but, for reasons which are His, God has decreed that *the way* in which this redemption is to be appropriated by the individual is the way of faith. "Whosoever *believeth* . . . shall not perish." "He that believeth *not* . . . is condemned already." It is not for us to delve into the whys and wherefores which prompted God to decree that faith should be the channel whereby men accept His universal amnesty. It is for us only to look into His Word and ask: Does He really say so? And anyone who can read will agree He does.[2]

Admitting once more that human analogies are always weak and never do justice to the divine situation which they seek to describe, we shall use an actual historical incident to throw light on the point which we are making. In 1829 two men, Wilson and Porter, were convicted of murder while robbing the United States mails and sentenced to death by hanging. Three weeks before the time set for Wilson's execution he was pardoned by President Andrew Jackson. To the surprise and

[2] *Acts 16:31; Romans 3:23-28; 5:1; Galatians 2:16; Ephesians 2:8.*

consternation of all, Wilson refused the pardon. The case went to the Supreme Court, and the Court finally handed down the following decision: "A pardon is a deed, to the validity of which delivery is essential, and delivery is not complete without acceptance. It may be rejected by the person to whom it is tendered; and if it is rejected, we have discovered no power in this court to force it upon him."

The amnesty which Christ has won for every member of the human family can be rejected in only one way: through unbelief. And similarly it can be accepted and made our own in only one way: through belief. The prisoner who has received the good news of his pardon and has seen the governor's signature and seal attesting to its validity has only one thing to do in order to receive the freedom which it offers: believe it! His mere believing, to be sure, will in no way bring about his pardon; but, once his pardon has been secured and delivered, his believing will make the blessings of the pardon his. The pardon, of course, must be *there* before belief in the pardon can do him any good. The Christian message tells us that through Christ our pardon is — there!

Right here we have come to that distinctive doctrine of Christian revelation which is known as "justification by faith." Frankly, we wish that there were a different word that we could use in the place of that forbidding, technical expression. While we were at the seminary, we delighted in the term "justification," and during the years in which we occupied a pulpit we used it in almost every sermon. Having spent a goodly portion of our life since then in the company of the common man, we are convinced that the Latin word "justification" is Greek to ninety per cent of the non-churchgoing public and perhaps even to the majority of those who are classified as churchgoing. And yet the idea which this expression was originally intended to convey is, in a sense, the pivot on which the entire Christian revelation rests. In a very real sense the whole Bible was written to tell man that he is "justified by faith."

Now, just what does that mean?

Throughout the centuries men have been conscious of the fact that there was something wrong in their relationship to God. Sometimes, it is true, this consciousness was only vague. At other times it was pointed, painful, and distressing. The consciousness of not being "right" with God has driven millions to distraction, others to insanity, and still others to horrible deeds of self-torture and even self-destruction. Indeed, most of what we call "religion" today has grown from the innate consciousness of man that something must be done to establish a right relationship between him and a higher Being — a Being to whom, he knows, he is responsible for everything he thinks and says and does.

According to Christian revelation this gnawing consciousness is the result of sin. Because of his rebellion against God, man is afraid to step into the presence of his Maker. By a divinely implanted intuition he knows that his has been a life of transgression of the holy will, and he knows that sin can never stand in the presence of holiness. And so, instinctively, he cringes. In the face of God's righteousness, how will he ever be able to stand on the Day of Judgment?

Throughout the recorded history of man, *natural* religion has given one of two (or a combination of both) answers to this question. The first: win the favor of the gods, that is, "get right" with them, by sacrifices and penances. The second: win their favor by a life of moral rectitude which even the gods will feel they must reward.

Speaking broadly, the former is the religion of the pagan world; and the latter is the religion of the so-called "Christian" world inasfar as it has departed from the message of Biblical revelation. Neither of these two answers is the answer of the Scriptures. They are both the answer of natural man.

To the question: How does sinful man become right with God? the Christian religion has an answer utterly unique, utterly different from the answer of natural religion. To the Christian there is absolutely nothing that he can do to make himself right with God. No penances, no sacrifices, no prayers, no rituals, no works, no morality, no righteousness, no goodness. Nothing. According to the Christian religion, if a man is ever to be made right with God, it will have to be God who does the righting.

This act, whereby an individual is "made right" with God, the Bible calls "justification." It is God who re-establishes the right relationship between the individual and Himself. And He does this by justifying him, that is, *by declaring him just and righteous* — in view of the substitutionary sacrifice of Jesus Christ, His Son. Justification, in its simplest terms, is the declaration of God that He is willing to look upon Mary Jones and Bill Smith as completely righteous in His sight — not because of anything that Mary or Bill have done, but because of the universal amnesty which Christ has won for them through the payment of His Cross.

And how can Mary and Bill be sure that God *has* declared them righteous in view of Christ's atonement? Only by faith. Only by believing. By believing what God has told them in the pages of divine revelation. Faith, as it were, is the hand by which man reaches up and accepts the divine

receipt, the "Paid in Full" of the Christian Gospel.
Faith is not a human virtue which God rewards
with the blessings of salvation; faith is rather the
reaching out of an empty hand into which God
places the gift of our redemption. Faith has nothing to add to what Christ has already done; it has
only to receive what, in His mercy, Christ has
already accomplished by the victory of His Cross.

The Bible puts it this way: We have been
"justified freely (that is, without price) by His
grace (that is, by God's undeserved love) through
the redemption that is in Christ Jesus (that is,
through the great act of atonement on the cross),
whom God hath foreordained to be a Propitiation
(that is, a payment) through *faith* in His blood
(that is, His death on the cross)." [3] And just a few
verses later: "Therefore, being justified by *faith*,
we have peace with God through our Lord Jesus
Christ, by whom also we have access by *faith* into
this grace wherein we stand, and rejoice in hope
of the glory of God." [4] In short, it is by faith that
we come into possession of every spiritual blessing
which Christ has won for us by the glorious triumph
of His Cross.

Scripture speaks of this justification of the sinner
before God under two different aspects. In the one
instance it speaks of justification as taking some-

[3] *Romans 3:24, 25.*        [4] *Romans 5:1, 2.*

thing away from the sinner, namely, his sin and guilt. In the other instance it speaks of justification as placing something to the sinner's credit, namely, the righteousness of Christ. Let us say a few words about these two aspects of the Bible doctrine of justification.

In the Epistle to the Colossians we are told that Christ "blotted out the handwriting . . . that was against us . . . and took it out of the way, nailing it to His cross." [5] Again and again, as in this passage, the Bible pictures humanity as hopelessly in debt to God because of sin. There is in heaven, as it were, an unpayable I. O. U. against every human soul — his unpayable moral debt to his Maker. As long as that debt remains unpaid, sinful man must remain forever separated from the Holy Presence. But Christ, the Bible tells us, "blotted out the handwriting . . . that was against us . . . and took it out of the way, nailing it to His cross." Christ by His atonement has removed the charges which stood against us. God has canceled all accounts. Because of the payment of God's Son, God has wiped the slate clean. God has "justified" the sinner. That is the first aspect of justification — a taking away of the load of guilt.

But God has not only canceled something which stood as a debit in the hopeless account of man;

[5] *Colossians 2:14.*

He has also entered something which will stand as an eternal credit. He has written the righteousness of His Son into the credit column of all who believe in Him. The Bible speaks of God as "imputing righteousness." [6] to the sinner who has no righteousness of his own. St. Paul, as we stated in a previous chapter, spoke of having no righteousness of his own but one which was his by faith in Christ.[7] And he also spoke, in another place, of the perfect righteousness of Christ as having been entered by God to the credit of the entire human family.[8] This is another aspect of the Bible's doctrine of justification. God imputes (credits) the righteousness of Christ to the unrighteous sinner who comes to him in faith.

But what does all this mean? Just how does it work?

Perhaps we can best illustrate the significance of this aspect of Christian revelation by recalling the story of the man who attended his first 3-D movie. Not knowing that the picture which he was about to see would be projected in three dimensions, he had not stopped to take the pair of glasses which were offered free of charge in the lobby. When the picture was thrown on the screen, he was surprised and puzzled by the hazy jumble

---

[6] *Romans 4:6, 24.*    [7] *Philippians 3:9.*
[8] *Romans 5:17-19.*

which he saw. Noticing that everyone around him was wearing a special pair of glasses, supplied by the management, he asked the usher for a pair. As soon as he looked at the screen through these glasses, the jumbled haze became a beautiful picture.

In His unsearchable wisdom, God has chosen to look at the penitent believer — through Christ! Besmirched by sin though the believer may be, God chooses to see him in that glorious dimension made possible by the righteousness of His own beloved Son. Or, as the Bible puts it, God sees the penitent believer "in Christ." The penitent believer is fully covered, fully clothed in the imputed righteousness of his Savior, a righteousness which has been written to *his* account! God, as it were, does not see the unrighteousness of the sinner; He sees the righteousness of Christ which He has thrown around the penitent. Clothed in that perfect righteousness, a righteousness which is not his own, the sinner can stand in the presence of his Maker.[9]

The poet conveys this thought beautifully in the lines:

Jesus, Thy blood and righteousness,
My beauty are, my glorious dress,
Wherein before my God I'll stand
When I shall reach the heavenly land.

[9] *Romans 3:20-22; 4:22-24; 5:17-19.*

According to the Christian revelation, then, God has provided a perfect righteousness, with which He is willing to cover and to clothe His fallen creatures — the perfect righteousness of Christ, which He is willing to write to the sinner's credit.

Perhaps these two aspects of the sinner's justification in God's sight — the removal of his debt and the crediting of his account — can be illustrated by the following historical incident. It is said that at one time in his life Henry Clay owed $10,000 to a bank in Kentucky. A number of sympathetic friends, knowing that Mr. Clay was troubled over his inability to pay, secretly raised the money and quietly paid off the debt.

When Mr. Clay later came to the bank to discuss his large indebtedness, the cashier startled him with the unexpected announcement: "Mr. Clay, you don't owe this bank a cent. Your account has been paid in full." "Why, how am I to understand you?" Mr. Clay exclaimed. "Well," said the cashier, "a number of your friends have raised a sufficient sum and have paid off your debt for you. You don't owe this bank a thing." Tears rushed into Mr. Clay's eyes, and, unable to speak, he walked away. His heart was overwhelmed by the joy of a great deliverance — deliverance from a crushing debt.

When Mr. Clay went to bed that night, he knew that, at long last, he was "right" with his bank. Not because of anything that he had done, but because of something someone *else* had done — and because that "something" had been written to his credit.

"Even as David also describeth the blessedness of the man unto whom God imputeth righteousness without works, saying, Blessed are they whose iniquities are forgiven and whose sins are covered. Blessed is the man to whom the Lord will not impute sin." [10]

[10] *Romans 4:6, 7.*

## XII

## THE WAY OF LIFE

As so frequently happens on a movie lot, an actor came to us one day and objected to the lines which we had written into the script. In the margins he had scribbled what he considered an improvement on our dialog.

The plot involved the story of a man who had become guilty of a serious crime against society. For months he had brooded over his guilt, and it seemed that he would lose his mind unless he found "release." It was at a moment when his remorse had reached its lowest depth that a Christian friend assured him: "Bill, I don't care what you did, or how terrible it was — God has forgiven you, for Jesus' sake. If you'll only believe Him."

In the opinion of our actor friend we were making it too easy for the criminal. "Why, if you let a line like that go out over television, you'll be encouraging every criminal in the country to go out and kill as often as he wants to. All he needs to do is believe that God has already forgiven him!"

What our good friend was forgetting was that Christianity is not only a way of faith, it is also a way of life. The man who really believes that God has forgiven him because of the sacrifice of His Son on the cross is not the man who is going to "go out and kill as often as he wants to." And why not? Because something *happens* to the man who really believes. The Apostle Paul, who, by divine inspiration, wrote a large part of the New Testament, was keenly aware of this possible misunderstanding of the Christian message. After writing at length in his Epistle to the Romans about the total depravity of man and about the total grace of God, who stands ready to forgive for the Savior's sake, Paul starts his sixth chapter with the question:

"Now, what is our response to be? Shall we sin to our heart's content and see how far we can exploit the grace of God? What a ghastly thought! We who have died to sin — how could we live in sin a moment longer?" [1] And a few verses farther on he asks: "Shall we go on sinning because we have no Law to condemn us any more, but are living under grace? Never! Just think what it would mean. You *belong* to the power which you choose to obey, whether you choose sin, whose reward is death, or God, obedience to whom means the re-

[1] *Romans 6:1, 2. P.*

ward of righteousness. Thank God that you, who were at one time the servants of Sin, honestly responded to the impact of Christ's teaching when you came under its influence. Then, released from the service of Sin, you entered the service of righteousness. [I use an everyday illustration because human nature grasps truth more readily that way.] . . . Sin *pays* its servants: the wage is death. But God *gives* to those who serve Him: His free gift is eternal life through Jesus Christ, our Lord." [2]

The point Paul is making in the above passage is this: Along with the acceptance of divine forgiveness through Christ goes a complete change of allegiance; servants of Sin become servants of God. And servants of God don't "go out and kill as often as they want to"! Servants of God serve God's purposes. In another place Paul writes: "He died for all, that they which live should not henceforth live unto themselves, but unto Him which died for them and rose again." [3] And a few verses later: "If any man be in Christ, he is a new creature; old things are passed away; behold, all things are become new." [4]

In other words, the man who has stepped into a new relationship with God through faith in the Cross of Christ has, as a matter of literal fact, be-

[2] *Romans 6:15-23. P.*     [3] *2 Corinthians 5:15.*
[4] *2 Corinthians 5:17.*

come a new creature. God has given him a new
heart. God has given him a new life, a new purpose, a new incentive for living, a new power to
live by, new tastes, new appetites — new everything!
He is a new creation, created by God's Holy Spirit.
If ever there was a man who became a new creature after he learned the meaning of Christ's Cross,
that man was Paul himself. Listen to what this
former persecutor of the Church has to say for
himself:

"Every advantage that I had gained I considered lost for Christ's sake. Yes, and I look upon
everything as loss compared with the overwhelming gain of knowing Christ Jesus, my Lord. For
His sake I did in actual fact suffer the loss of everything, but I considered it useless rubbish compared
with being able to win Christ. For now my place
is in Him, and I am not dependent upon any of
the self-achieved righteousness of the Law. God
has given me that genuine righteousness which
comes from faith in Christ. *How changed are my
ambitions!* . . . Yet, my brothers, I do not consider
myself to have 'arrived,' spiritually, nor do I consider myself already perfect. But I keep going on,
grasping ever more firmly that purpose for which
Christ grasped me. My brothers, I do not consider
myself to have fully grasped it even now. But I do
concentrate on this: I leave the past behind and

with hands outstretched to whatever lies ahead I go straight for the goal — my reward, the honor of being called by God in Christ." [5]

Now, it so happens that the man who wrote those words *had* at one time in his life gone out to see how many Christians he could round up and bring to the city of Jerusalem for execution.[6] Indeed, "how changed were his ambitions"! Surely, here was a "new creature." Here was a man with a new allegiance. No longer a "servant of Sin," but a "servant of God."

How do you explain the change-over?

Once again, let Paul do his own explaining. In his Letter to the Galatians he writes: "I am crucified with Christ; nevertheless I live; yet not I, but Christ liveth in me; and the life which I now live in the flesh I live by the faith of the Son of God, who loved me and gave Himself for me." [7] Somehow, in the center of Paul's life there was a power which drove him on and on to ever greater heights of Christian living; and that power was the Cross of Jesus Christ. As an electric motor, reduced to its simplest terms, is but a series of responses of a moving body to a stationary magnet, so the life of the believer is a series of endless responses to the magnetic power of Christ's Cross. That Cross, the Bible says, is "the power of God." [8]

[5] *Philippians 3:7-14. P.*     [6] *Acts 9:1, 2.*
[7] *Galatians 2:20.*     [8] *1 Corinthians 1:18.*

The power of Christ's Cross exerts its magnetism upon the life of the believer both in a general and in a particular manner. To illustrate the former, we shall recount the following by way of an analogy. During the early days of the past century a wealthy plantation owner of the South was attracted by the heart-breaking sobs of a slave girl who was about to step up to the auction block. Moved by a momentary impulse of generosity, he bought her at a very high price and then disappeared, mysteriously, into the crowd which thronged the auction place. When the auction was over, the clerk came to the sobbing girl and handed her her bill of sale. To her astonishment, the plantation owner had written "Free" over the paper which should have delivered her to him as his possession. She stood stunned and speechless, as one by one the other slaves were claimed by their owners and dragged away. Suddenly, she threw herself at the feet of the clerk and exclaimed: "Where is the man who bought me? I must find him! He has set me free! I must serve him all the rest of my life!"

"He has set me *free* — I must *serve* him!" That is the power which the Cross of Christ exerts over the life of the believer. By establishing a new relationship between man and God, a relationship of grace, the Cross is a constant motive power in the heart of the Christian, impelling him to ever higher levels of Christian virtue. "The love of Christ constraineth us," Paul says.[9] Or, as Phillips paraphrases this well-known verse, "The very spring of our actions is the love of Christ." The Christian life is, as it were, a river which, if traced to its source high up on the mountainside, will be found to bubble from a spring at the foot of the Cross. Subconsciously, there is always that drive — down deep in the heart of every Christian — "He has set me *free* — I must *serve* Him!" And in that service the way of faith becomes the way of life.

But the Cross of Christ exerts its influence upon the life of the Christian also in a very particular manner. Not only does it affect his life as a whole; it also affects his individual thoughts and words and deeds. The Christian can make no moral decision unless, consciously or subconsciously, he relates that decision to the Cross of Christ. Is he perhaps called upon to help a man in need? "The love of Christ constraineth him." Is he asked to make sacrifices of time, energy, money, and convenience to give his children a thorough Christian training? "The love of Christ constraineth him." As a Christian he really has no choice other than to respond to the love of Christ poured out on Calvary's cross.

And, conversely, is he tempted to repay evil with evil? Is he tempted to curse, to use ill-

9 *2 Corinthians 5:14.*

tempered or even profane language? Is he tempted
to cheat, to defraud, to lie, to hate, to envy, to
slander, to steal, to be loveless, unkind, uncharitable?
The love of Christ constrains him *not* to! It was
Sin, our Sin, that brought Him to His Cross. It
was Love, Christ's Love, that canceled out our Sin.
How can we repay that Love with base ingratitude?
A seventeenth-century poet gave eloquent expression to this restraining power of the Cross when he
wrote:

> Grant that I Thy Cross may view
>     With repentant grieving,
> Nor Thee crucify anew
>     By unholy living.
> How could I refuse to shun
>     Every sinful pleasure,
> Since for me God's only Son
>     Suffered without measure!

The Christian message is not only a way of
faith. It is also a way of *life* — a way of life which
draws its power from the message of the Cross.
Throughout the centuries there have been millions,
and there are multiplied millions today, who have
taken their stand with the great Apostle Paul and
have asserted to an uncomprehending world: "The
life which I now live in the flesh I live by the faith
of the Son of God, who loved me and gave Himself
for me." [10]

[10] *Galatians 2:20.*

## XIII

## THE WAY OF HOPE

The other night we stood at the sickbed of our fourteen-year-old niece. She didn't know — but the rest of us who stood at her bedside did — that before the week was up, she would very probably fall into her final sleep. She was sure that her illness was only "a rare kind of anemia," but her parents and friends knew that it was leukemia. In fact, it was just that day that the doctor had told the parents that medical science could hold out no hope. A few days more — and the dread disease would take its toll. As, indeed, it did only two days later.

What could we say to the distressed mother as we drove her from the hospital to our home that evening? Surely nothing that had happened in the past few days had made any sense at all. Nathalie had been an "A" student in her freshman year at high school, had excelled in athletics, and showed promise in the field of music. Only four weeks ago she had romped in the vigor and bloom of youth, as carefree as any of her classmates. Tonight she lay limp — in the pallor of approaching death.

How could anyone make these things add up? We thought of the dozens of "get-well" cards which lay on her bedside table with their well-meant but baseless wishes. Whistles in the dark — all of them! We thought of a seventy-four-year-old cousin who lay paralyzed in a Cleveland hospital, where she has lain half dead, half alive, for more than twenty years. At seventy-four she is still alive and may live for many years more. But little Nathalie would die — before the week was out. Could anyone make rhyme or reason out of *that?*

Could there be a God in heaven who would permit such things to happen? And if so, does He rub His hands in ghoulish glee as He snuffs out the life of helpless children and breaks the hearts of pleading parents? Is He an ogre? A fiend? A heartless monster who, although He has the power to change the tragic destiny of men, refuses to use that power in man's behalf?

Above all, is it possible, in the face of stark and bitter tragedy, to speak of a God of *love?*

It would *not* be possible — if there had been no Cross!

As we drove home from the hospital that evening, we quoted a verse of Scripture to the grief-stricken mother, a verse which, for us, has assumed more and more significance with every passing year.

It is a statement of St. Paul. "What shall we say to these things?" he asks. And then he answers: "If God be for us, who can be against us? He that spared not His own Son, but delivered Him up for us all, how shall he not with Him also freely give us all things?" [1]

There were a lot of things we couldn't understand that night. But there was one thing we as Christians did know — beyond the possibility of doubt. Above us, reigning in His heavens, was a God who was *for us*. Above us was a God of love. Not just a God of love in general, but a God who had demonstrated His love for us in one supreme act of self-revelation — the death of His only-begotten Son in our behalf. In that one great cosmic act He had proved, once and for all time, that He is for us. He is definitely and assuredly on our side. And, as the Bible puts it, "If God be for us, who can be against us? He that spared not His own Son, but delivered Him up for us all, how shall He not with Him also freely give us all things?" [2]

The Bible's logic is simply this: If God has given us the Gift, surely He will also let us have the ribbons. If He has given us His Son to die for us, to ransom us from the powers of Sin and Death, and to win us back to eternal fellowship with Him, then surely He'll find a way for us to surmount all

[1] *Romans 8:31, 82.*    [2] *Romans 8:32.*

of life's minor tragedies. If He has done the greater thing, surely He will do the smaller.

The Cross of Christ is the only basis, the only sure foundation, of Christian hope. Indeed, it is the only ground for prevailing hope that God has given to man. For it is only in the Cross of Christ that man can finally become convinced of God's mercy and His love. Where else can men turn for an authentic revelation of His love? The towering mountains and the billowing seas may tell us of His power. The sun and the moon and the rolling canopy of heaven may tell us of His wisdom. The test tube and the microscope may tell us of the marvelous secrets which He has tucked away in His material universe. But nowhere can we find incontrovertible evidence of His love — except in His own self-revelation through the Cross. It is there that we learn what God thinks of us, how He feels toward us, and what His intentions with us are.

Are we dealing here with some theological abstraction, of interest only to theologians? By no means. We are dealing with a pivotal truth which has a lively bearing on the life of the common man and woman every hour of the day. To go through life without the assurance of God's love would be nothing but a ghastly nightmare. Who would want to get up in the morning and go to work, not knowing how God felt toward him — not knowing if in

His holiness and righteousness God had thrown him off forever! Who would want to slave at the office or sweat at the work bench or ironing board, or who would want to go to bed another night — not knowing if the God into whose presence he may step by morning is a hateful monster or a merciful and loving Father!

Indeed, nothing is more important in life than to know that God loves us, and nowhere can we find that assurance but in the Cross of Christ. It is at the Cross that we learn that "God is Love." [3] It is at the Cross that we are assured that "God so loved the world." [4] Without the Cross and its revelation of the Father heart of God, who could know? "To us," says the Bible, "the greatest demonstration of God's love for us has been His sending His only Son into the world to give us Life through Him. We see real love, not in the fact that we loved God, but that He loved us and sent His Son to make personal atonement for our sins." [5] To the Bible writers, the Cross was the pivotal point in human history where divine love came down to cope with human need.

Perhaps right here we should recount another personal experience. We were seated on the stage one day discussing the plot of the television story we were filming. The man with whom we were

[3] 1 John 4:8.　　[4] John 3:16.
[5] 1 John 4:9, 10. P.

talking was not too impressed by the point we were trying to make in this particular episode. "After all," he said, "you don't mean to tell me that a Christian is any better prepared to face sudden disappointment or a prolonged and painful tragedy than is any other deeply religious person." We had to tell him: "Yes, we do mean that." Not every person who is merely "religious," no matter how deeply, knows for sure that God loves him, and unless he can come to that assurance, he is not prepared to stand up under the repeated blows of adversity. He may say glibly that he knows God loves him, but he *can't* know for sure unless or until he takes God's own Word for it — and God's own Word, in this instance, is the Cross of His Son. "The proof of God's amazing love is this . . . that Christ died for us!" says Paul.[6] He who rejects that proof can never be sure.

We have no bone to pick with the greeting-card industry. They are doing a magnificent job. But there is something tragically hollow about the assurance of many a card which is classified under "Shut In" and "Cheer" and "Get Well." In many instances their wishes are rooted in a baseless optimism. Who has any warrant to say that "everything is going to turn out fine"? Frequently things *don't* turn out fine! Who has any warrant to say

[6] *Romans 5:8. P.*

that "all things work together for good"? Frequently
they don't. There can be no ultimate assurance of
any lasting good in this world, unless that assurance
is rooted in God. And to be rooted in God means
to be rooted in Christ. And to be rooted in Christ
means to accept His Cross as the ultimate assurance that God is gracious and good and that His
dealings with us are dictated by His love.

It simply is not true that all things work together for good for all people. When the Bible
says: "All things work together for good," it goes
to great pains to describe the people of whom that
is true. They are the people who have entrusted
their entire lives to the love of God as it has been
revealed through the Cross of Christ. To them, all
things, even death and bereavement, work together
for good, because their eternal destiny is to live in
blissful fellowship with God. That the Bible does
not promise that all things will work together for
good for all people is evident from the following
words of Paul: "For there are many, of whom
I have told you before and tell you again now,
even with tears, that they are the enemies of the
Cross of Christ. These men are heading for *utter
destruction* — their god is their own appetite, their
pride is in what they should be ashamed of, and
this world is the limit of their horizon. But we are
citizens of heaven. Our outlook goes beyond this

world to the hopeful expectation of the Savior, who will come from heaven, the Lord Jesus Christ." [7] To Paul, and to the other Bible writers, the believers in the Cross of Christ and the *dis*believers in that Cross are two entirely different kinds of people — headed for two entirely different destinies. To the believers, all things must work together for good, because the scattered and broken lines of their lives must converge ultimately upon the returning Christ. To the disbeliever, nothing can ultimately work for his good, since he is "heading for destruction."

These great and fundamental truths find their daily application in the lives of all believers. The Cross and its message of divine love is an endless reservoir of hope in every circumstance of life. If we can say so without seeming irreverent, the Cross and its message is God's eternal greeting card addressed to His beloved. And it is suited to all occasions. Its message in all cases is simply this: "Cheer up! God loves you!" Is business bad? Is employment hard to get? Are the bills piling high? Has a loved one been in the hospital for weeks and months? Are we far from home and lonely? Does the world seem to pass us by? Have our friends begun to consider us expendable? Are we having trouble at home, at school, at the shop, at the

[7] *Philippians 3:18-20. P.*

office? Is our marriage an unhappy one? Is some sickness or malignancy eating at our body, and is death, which seemed so far away only a few months ago, coming closer and closer? — There stands the Cross of Christ, the revelation of God's endless mercy. And its message? "Cheer up! God loves you!" And since God loves you, He will see to it that all things — even *this* — will work together for your good.

Hope is almost a theme word of the New Testament. And invariably it is associated, in some way or another, with the Cross of Christ — His death in the place of sinners. To the Romans Paul says: "Being justified by faith . . . we rejoice in hope." [8] That is, being delivered from the power of Sin and Death through faith in the atonement of the Savior, we revel in the hope which God has poured into our hearts. And hope here is not a pious wish, it is rather a sure confidence. It is the sure confidence of which Paul speaks throughout the eighth chapter of his Letter to the Romans. Listen to these few extracts from that marvelous chapter:

"We *know* that all things work together for good to them that love God, to them who are the called according to His purpose. . . . If God be for us, who can be against us? He that spared not His own Son, but delivered Him up for us all, how shall He not with Him also freely give us *all*

[8] *Romans 5:1, 2.*

things? . . . Who shall separate us from the love of Christ? Shall tribulation or distress or persecution or famine or nakedness or peril or sword? . . . Nay, in all these things we are more than conquerors through Him that loved us. For I am persuaded that neither death nor life nor angels nor principalities nor powers nor things present nor things to come nor height nor depth nor any other creature shall be able to separate us from the love of God which is in Christ Jesus, our Lord." [9]

For Paul, the love of God on which he based his hope was inseparably tied up with Christ Jesus, his Lord — that great Savior who had died that he might live.

What the message of the Cross means to the Christian hope is beautifully brought out in the well-known words of Sir John Bowring:

> When the woes of life o'ertake me,
> Hopes deceive and fears annoy,
> Never shall the Cross forsake me:
> Lo! It glows with peace and joy.
>
> When the sun of bliss is beaming
> Light and love upon my way,
> From the Cross, the radiance streaming
> Adds more luster to the day.
>
> Bane and blessing, pain and pleasure,
> By the Cross are sanctified;
> Peace is there that knows no measure,
> Joys that through all time abide.

[9] *Romans 8:28-39.*

## XIV

## THE CROSS IS THE KEY

Every clergyman will recognize the familiar refrain. It would be humorous if it were not so tragic, so desperately tragic! "Yes, sir, Reverend, I've got my own religion. I'm doing what the Good Book says. The Ten Commandments, the Sermon on the Mount, the Golden Rule — these are all I need. It's like I always say, if only everybody else would do like me. . . ."

There is only one element of truth in that familiar bromide. The man who speaks it *does* have his own religion. It is definitely not the religion of Christian revelation. It is not the religion of the Bible. It is rather the religion of the natural heart. A church census conducted in a western city some years ago revealed that the overwhelming majority of the people interviewed agreed that their religion, when reduced to its essential content, was basically an observance of the Golden Rule. They believed that if we do unto others as we would

have them do unto us, then God will do unto us
as we have done unto others. In other words, they
believed that their happiness in the hereafter would
be dependent upon how they observed the Golden
Rule in the here and now.

That is not surprising. Because of the great number of faiths which have been absorbed into our
national culture, including not only the three so-
called major faiths, Protestant, Roman Catholic, and
Jewish, but also the more than two hundred sects
which are commonly classified under the general
head of "Protestant" — because of this conglomera-
tion of religious beliefs, our magazines and news-
papers have occasionally limited their religious pro-
nouncements to those parts of Scripture which are
least likely to offend their readers. Like motherhood
and patriotism, everyone is in favor of the Ten
Commandments, the Sermon on the Mount, and the
Golden Rule. And so these are the elements of
Scripture which have been quoted again and again
not only in the public press, on the political plat-
form, and in the chambers of government, but also
in the everyday face-to-face conversations of the
average man and woman. It is not surprising, therefore, that in the minds of many people Christianity
has been made equivalent to the Ten Commandments, the Sermon on the Mount, and the Golden
Rule.

Now, it is true of course that these three price-less statements are a part of Christian revelation. They are an integral and an important part of the inspired Scriptures. But to speak of them as being the equivalent of Christianity is to be as wrong as the blind man of Hindustan who, holding the tail of an elephant, insisted: "Methinks, an elephant is very like a rope." There was a lot more to the ele-phant than he thought. And there is a lot more to the Christian religion than the Golden Rule.

Indeed, the Golden Rule, if taken out of its rela-tion to the entire Scripture, can be disastrous to the man who puts his trust in it. The Ten Command-ments, if they are made a way to heaven, can only lead to hell. The Sermon on the Mount holds out no hope, no comfort, no assurance to the man who has ever been proud, unmerciful, or impure of heart. If we may be permitted an analogy, we would refer to certain potent chemicals which, if mixed in proper proportion to other ingredients, are indeed a bless-ing to humanity. But if taken alone, they are sure to result in sudden death. Similarly there are parts of divine revelation which, if taken in their relation to the entire Christian message, are bound to pro-duce their divinely intended purpose and in the end will result in good for humankind. But if taken alone and used for any other than their intended purpose, they can only result in death — death for the soul of man. The Golden Rule, the Ten Commandments, and the Sermon on the Mount are such ingredients of God's over-all message to man. They dare never be taken out of their divinely intended relation to the Cross, the center of *all* revelation.

We are extremely reluctant to propose a key to the understanding of the Scriptures. First, because such proposals usually smack of presumption. Who are *we* to offer keys to the understanding of God's Holy Word? Secondly, because some who have offered keys to the Scriptures have succeeded only in locking them. Keys, as you know, can work both ways. They can open, and they can close. Let anyone who proposes to offer the world a key to Scripture, therefore, be sure that the key which he is offering is to be found in the Scriptures themselves and not in his own imaginings.

Anyone who reads the Bible and takes its words as they read, especially the Epistles of St. Paul, will see that the Christian revelation gravitates, as it were, around two poles. These two great poles of Christian doctrine the Bible calls the Law [1] and the Gospel. [2] Until a man has learned to distinguish between these two, he is not likely to find much harmony in the Scriptures and, what is worse, he is in constant danger of using the Bible to his hurt. The Apostle Peter speaks of "ill-informed people"

[1] *Galatians 3:10-13.*     [2] *Romans 1:16.*

who "distort" the Scriptures and who, in doing so, "bring disaster on their own heads." [3] There has been no greater distortion of the Bible than the tragic confusion of Law and Gospel.

Well, what *is* the Law? And what *is* the Gospel? And why is it so dangerous to mix or to confuse the two? And where does the Cross of Jesus Christ come into this picture?

The word "law," of course, is familiar to us from our everyday living. There are thousands of laws on the statute books of our nation, as well as of our several states, counties, and cities. These laws tell us what we are to do and not to do, and in many instances they stipulate the penalty which will follow their transgression. We have traffic laws, trade laws, sanitation laws, tax laws, and laws of all descriptions. Characteristic of all of them is their monotonous repetition of dos and don'ts. Had they been written in an earlier period of the development of the English language, they would have been stated in a series of "thou shalts" and "thou shalt nots." "Thou shalt not drive more than so or so many miles an hour," for instance.

Now, certain portions of the Bible are also devoted to Law. These are the laws of God. These, too, tell us what we are to do and not to do. And these, too, stipulate a penalty for their transgres-

[3] *2 Peter 3:16. P.*

sion.[4] Nor are these divine directives restricted to the Ten Commandments. Any passage of Scripture which tells unconverted humanity how it is to behave and which tells the unregenerate to "do this" or "do that" is Law. And similarly, any passage of Scripture which holds out heaven as a reward for righteous living, either expressly or by implication, is Law. Thus, for instance, the Golden Rule is Law! It tells us what to do. So, too, is the Sermon on the Mount. So, too, are the Ten Commandments. So, too, are a hundred and one other statements of the Scripture which prescribe a code for moral living and which, expressly or by implication, hold out heaven as a reward for a moral life. These all are Law.

Now, the overwhelmingly important fact is that the Bible insists that no man can keep the Law of God. Again and again the Bible fairly shouts that no man can be rescued from the power of Sin and Death by the keeping of the Law — not by the keeping of the Ten Commandments nor the Golden Rule nor the Sermon on the Mount nor any other moral precept of the Scriptures! Paul keeps harping on this fact almost constantly throughout his Epistles. He uses the word "Law" no fewer than ninety-six times, and very frequently he is speaking of the Law in contrast to the Gospel. Usually he is

4 *Galatians 3:10-13.*

pointing out that the Law never has saved, never will, and never *can* save any man. Sometimes Paul gives us the impression of a man who has been sent out by the city to erect "Street Does Not Run Through" signs at the entrance to blind alleys. To Paul, as well as to other Bible writers, the Law is a blind alley. Those who enter it will find it boarded up at the first turn. It does not run through to heaven. In fact, Paul makes it very clear that the Law, if pursued to its bitter end, is a highway that ends in hell.

The man who really believes that he can merit release from the powers of Sin and Death by his observance of the Law and who really wants to act on that belief must keep the Law in all its parts. And that, the Bible claims, is utterly impossible. Listen to these words of Scripture: "No man can justify himself before God by a perfect performance of the Law's demands; indeed it is the straight-edge of the Law that shows us how crooked we are." [5] Or again: "The Law never succeeded in producing righteousness — the failure was always the weakness of human nature." [6] Nor will it do to keep ninety per cent of the Law, for the Bible says: "Whosoever shall keep the whole Law, and yet offend in one point, he is guilty of all." [7] Indeed, as a way to heaven the Bible considers the Law far *worse*

[5] *Romans 3:20. P.*          [6] *Romans 8:3. P.*
[7] *James 2:10.*

than a blind alley. It considers it a broken bridge whose center span has fallen into the river. No man can cross from earth to heaven by treading the path of the Law. No man can cross from earth to heaven by following a moral code, even though that code be the commandments of the Scriptures. He simply cannot keep them. That bridge is broken! Christ came to replace that bridge! And He replaced it with His Cross.

Perhaps in no book of the Bible are we shown more clearly the utter futility of trying to get to heaven by keeping the Law than in the Epistle to the Galatians. The Christians in Galatia had begun to straddle the issue, as if heaven could be gained both by trusting in the message of the Cross and by performing the works of the Law — both by faith in the atonement of Christ and by a moral life. What does Paul say to them? Listen! "O you dear idiots of Galatia (who saw Jesus Christ the Crucified so plainly), who has been casting a spell over you? I will ask you one simple question: Did you receive the Spirit of God by trying to keep the Law or by believing the message of the Gospel?" [8] He then proceeds to show them that they had been brought into spiritual fellowship with God not by trying to live up to the Law, not by "works of righteousness," but by believing the Gospel of the Cross of Christ.

[8] *Galatians 3:1, 2. P.*

That brings us to the other pole of Christian revelation, namely, the Gospel. In the original Greek, "Gospel" means simply "good news." As this word is used in the New Testament, it means a very specific piece of good news: the good news that God came down from heaven to earth in the Person of His Son to redeem all men from the curse of Sin and Death and to gain for them eternal access into the heavenly kingdom. Unlike the Law, the Gospel is not a directive. It is a message. It is the thrilling message of Chapter VI of this book: "Christ Victorious — Mankind Freed!" or of Chapter VIII: "Paid in Full— All Debts Are Canceled!" or of Chapter IX: "The Law Fulfilled — All Men Redeemed!" It is the good news which has the Cross at its center and which proclaims to all men everywhere that "God was in Christ, reconciling the world unto Himself, not imputing their trespasses unto them." [9]

The Gospel tells men whose backs are breaking under the stern requirements of the Law that Christ has redeemed them from the Law and its impossible demands. He has forever rescued them from its curse and punishment.[10] The Gospel tells men that, because of the supreme sacrifice of Christ upon the cross, in view of which God has settled all accounts, the sins of all men have been erased forever from

[9] *2 Corinthians 5:19.*　　　　[10] *Galatians 3:13; 4:4, 5.*

the memory of God. It tells men that, because of
the Cross, God can say: "Though your sins be as
scarlet, they shall be as white as snow; though they
be red like crimson, they shall be as wool." [11] The
Gospel tells all men everywhere that "the blood of
Jesus Christ, His Son, cleanseth us from all sin. . . .
And He is the Propitiation [reconciliation] for our
sins, and not for ours only, but also for the sins of
the whole world." [12] That — nothing more, nothing
less — is the Gospel. Jesus Himself gave us one of
the most beautiful summaries of the Gospel when
He said: "God so loved the world that He gave
His only-begotten Son, that whosoever believeth in
Him should not perish, but have everlasting life." [13]

The question naturally presents itself: How do
you reconcile the two — the Law and the Gospel?
Surely they are opposites! Surely they are opposed
to each other. In reply we say, yes, they are. They
are opposites. And they are opposed to each other.
But they are both part of God's divine revelation
to man. And they are both infinitely important in
God's plan for the conversion of the sinner and the
comfort of the saint. The proper distinction between
Law and Gospel is both extremely difficult and extremely simple. In our library we have an imposing
volume of 426 large pages printed in small type,

[11] *Isaiah 1:18.*          [12] *1 John 1:7—2:2.*
[13] *John 3:16.*

devoted entirely, from the first page to the last, to the proper distinction between these two doctrines of Scripture. It is entitled "Law and Gospel." We are thankful that in our seminary days we were required to read this book from cover to cover, for no man is ready to enter a Christian pulpit until he has learned to distinguish sharply between these two.

On the other hand, the distinction between these two parts of Christian revelation is not as difficult as it may at first seem. Long before we went to the seminary, in fact, when we were only twelve or thirteen years of age, we learned the fundamentals of the Christian faith from a little catechism. We shall never forget the answer to Question No. 101, which we were required to memorize already at that tender age. We shall repeat the question, and then we shall quote the answer:

"*Question:* What difference is there between the Law and the Gospel?"

"*Answer:*

"1. The Law teaches what *we* are to do and not to do; the Gospel teaches what *God* has done, and still does, for our salvation.

"2. The Law shows us our sin and the wrath of God; the Gospel shows us our Savior and the love of God.

"3. The Law demands, threatens, and condemns; the Gospel promises, gives, and seals unto us forgiveness, life, and salvation.

"4. The Law works wrath and kills; the Gospel invites and draws us to Christ, works faith, and thus gives us spiritual life.

"5. The Law must be preached to secure (unconcerned) sinners, the Gospel to such as are alarmed and terrified by their transgressions."

We shall comment only briefly on this classic answer. The primary purpose of the Law (including the Golden Rule!) is to show us our sin, and the primary purpose of the Gospel is to show us our Savior. The Bible tells us very much the same when it says: "Now, we know that what things soever the Law saith, it saith to them who are under the Law, that every mouth may be stopped and all the world become guilty before God. Therefore by the deeds of the Law shall no flesh be justified in His sight, for *by the Law is the knowledge of sin*." [14] If Paul were living today, he might have rendered this passage somewhat as follows: "The Law has placed all men into a relationship with God in which they must either 'put up' or 'shut up'; and since, because of their evil nature, they cannot 'put up,' all that is left for them to do is to 'shut up.' Everyone must silently admit his guilt

[14] *Romans 3:19, 20.*

before God. And so, as long as men remain in the relationship of the Law, they can never be justified in God's sight, because all that the Law can do for them is show them their *sins.*" Indeed, all that the Law can do toward the salvation of the sinner is show him his need of salvation through a means other than the Law. It is only when he finds Christ and His Gospel that he finally finds salvation.[15] That, in brief, is what our Catechism answer brings out in its first four points.

And now a look at Point Five. "The Law must be preached to secure (unconcerned) sinners, the Gospel to such as are alarmed and terrified by their transgressions." We have often marveled, when we went to our dentist, how he would lay out his tools on a tray before him and then how he would almost automatically always reach for the right tool as he became involved in the business of working on a filling or a bridge. There were perhaps a dozen tools, each with a specific function to perform. To us they all looked very much alike, but to the trained workman each was infinitely different from the others, and he used each for precisely the purpose for which it was intended. Perhaps few people realize that the trained workman in the holy ministry has also been entrusted with tools with varying purposes and that to use the wrong tool at the

15 *Romans 10:4; Galatians 2:21.*

wrong time, also in the Christian ministry, can eventuate in disaster. Paul cautioned a young minister of his day: "Study to show thyself approved unto God, a workman that needeth not to be ashamed, rightly dividing the Word of Truth." [16] The Christian minister or, for that matter, *any* Christian is to administer "the Word of Truth" with the intelligence and skill of the expert workman. He is to administer the Law where the Law is called for. And he is to speak the Gospel where hearts are ready for it.

The unconcerned sinner is not ready for the Gospel. He needs nothing so immediately and so sorely as the Law. He needs to be brought face to face with the demands of God's holiness. "Ye shall be holy, for I, the Lord, your God, am holy!" [17] "Be ye therefore perfect, even as your Father which is in heaven is perfect." [18] He needs to be brought face to face with the inexorable demands of God's justice, a justice which has already spoken a curse upon the life of the unconcerned and complacent sinner: "Cursed is everyone that continueth not in all things which are written in the Book of the Law to do them." [19] He needs to be brought to a realization that day after day he has smashed the Ten Commandments to "smithereens," has

[16] *2 Timothy 2:15.*
[17] *Leviticus 19:2.*
[18] *Matthew 5:48.*
[19] *Galatians 3:10.*

flouted the Golden Rule, has trampled the Sermon on the Mount under foot, and has shaken unholy fists of rebellion toward God in heaven. Not only must he be convicted of his guilt, but he must also be told of the punishment which God has decreed as commensurate with his guilt — spiritual death here and eternal death hereafter. He must be brought to cringe, to quake, and to quail under the stern rebuke of God's holy Law and under the dread prospect of an eternal separation from his Maker. He must be brought to cry out with the Apostle Paul: "O wretched man that I am! Who shall deliver me from this body of death?" [20] For then, and only then, will he be ready to hear from the lips of the Savior the wonderful Gospel assurance: "Son, be of good cheer, thy sins are forgiven thee." [21]

It would be spiritually fatal to preach the Gospel to a complacent sinner. He needs something else before he needs the Gospel. He needs the Law. And he needs the Law in all its severity. He needs to make the steep descent of the first four chapters of this book before he is ready to look up to the Cross of Christ and gain the comfort which it offers. He needs to make an agonizing reappraisal of his lost condition in the light of the holy Law of God.

[20] *Romans 7:24.*    [21] *Matthew 9:2.*

We are living in a day when men are inclined to pooh-pooh what they choose to call "hell-and-brimstone" preaching. Admitting that there may have been excesses in the past, particularly in the direction of cheap and extreme sensationalism, there *is* a type of hell-and-brimstone preaching which is an essential part of Bible Christianity. The preaching of the Law is always, in a sense, a type of hell-and-brimstone preaching. It is the proclaiming of the wrath of God against the sinfulness of men — not only of men in general but of individual men and women in particular. It is the proclaiming of a divine wrath from which the sinner can find refuge only in the Cross. It is a proclaiming of the *Law*, from whose terror the repentant sinner flees for comfort to the *Gospel*.

Indeed, the Cross of Christ, the doctrine of His atonement for the sins of all men everywhere, is the key to the entire Scripture. The Law, which man in his spiritual helplessness could never keep, made the Cross of Christ necessary. And the Cross, which God in His mercy provided as the only way out, made the Gospel possible.

## XV

## WISDOM OR NONSENSE?

It is, of course, a public secret that the Biblical message of the Cross is anything but popular today. This is true both inside and outside the established churches. Even though modern preaching still makes much of the Cross of Christ, and even though it still repeats many of the Biblical words and phrases in which the message was originally heralded, nevertheless in all too many instances it denies the very content which those words and phrases were intended to convey. In all too many instances it denies that when Jesus of Nazareth gave up His life on a Roman cross outside the city of Jerusalem, "God was in Christ, reconciling the world unto Himself, not imputing their trespasses unto them." [1] And in all too many instances it is reluctant to assert that when Jesus

[1] *2 Corinthians 5:19.*

Christ stepped forth from the grave on Easter morning, "He was declared to be the Son of God with power . . . by the resurrection from the dead." [2]

It will not do to speak of the death of Christ merely as a splendid example of self-sacrifice — the example of a brave and honorable man who would rather die than go back on his principles. It will not do to speak of the Cross merely as a tremendous moral influence which has exerted its ennobling effect on all succeeding generations. Of course, the Cross was that! But if that is all it was, then the entire document which tells us of the historical fact of the Cross is a hoax. Then the entire Scripture, both Old and New Testaments, is only a collection of superstitious myths, and the sooner we stop talking about the Bible as the inspired and infallible Word of God, the better. The Bible presents the Cross to man against the background of man's depravity and it proclaims the Cross as the instrument of man's deliverance from Sin and Death and Hell. Any cross which is less than that must be spelled with a small "c," for it is not the Cross of Scripture. It is the cross of man's invention.

It has been our good fortune to enjoy the personal friendship of some of America's denominational leaders, particularly those engaged in the field of mass communications. More than once, as

[2] *Romans 1:4.*

we lingered over a dinner with these good gentlemen, we became engaged in lively theological dis-
cussions. And more than once it became evident
how crucial — and how controversial — is this issue
of the Cross. In some theological circles there seems
to be a widespread allergy to the Biblical message
of redemption. There seems to be a squeamishness
over what some have chosen to call a "blood theology." Recently one of these denominational
leaders handed us a religious screenplay, intended
for national television release, which dealt specifically with the solution of a problem of guilt. The
screenplay already had denominational approval.
Nowhere in the entire script was the name of Christ
mentioned. Much less, of course, was there any
reference to His Cross. Nor, as we learned later,
was this omission due to an oversight.

When we went to college, our most distasteful
course was chemistry. But we do remember one
thing. If you have a liquid before you, and you
want to know whether it is an acid or a base, all
you need do is insert a piece of litmus paper into
the liquid. If litmus turns red, your liquid is an
acid. If litmus turns blue, you have a base. We
have learned in subsequent years that if you have
a man or a church body before you and you want
to determine whether or not their religion is Christian, all you need to do is dip the Cross of Christ

into their theology. Their reaction to the Cross will
be as infallible an index as the color of the litmus.
The Cross is the great revealer! When Mary and
Joseph brought the Infant Jesus into the Temple,
an old man named Simeon took the Infant into his
arms and, among other things, told Mary: "This
Child is set for the fall and rising again of many
in Israel and for a sign which shall be spoken
against. Yea, a sword shall pierce through thine
own soul also (at the time of her Son's crucifixion),
that the thoughts of many hearts may be revealed." [3]
It is the Cross — the message of God's rescue of the
human race through the emancipating death of His
beloved Son — that reveals men's thoughts and
divides them into two spiritually unassociated
groups.

This, of course, is nothing new. For various
reasons, men have always set themselves against
the Biblical message of the Cross. Listen to Paul
as he writes to a little group of Christians in
Corinth, at that time the largest city in Greece:
"I have no desire to rob the Cross of its power,"
he says. "The preaching of the Cross is, I know,
nonsense to those who are involved in this dying
world, but to us who are being saved from that
death it is nothing less than the power of God. It is
written: 'I will destroy the wisdom of the wise, and

[3] *Luke 2:34, 35.*

the prudence of the prudent will I reject.' For consider, what have the philosopher, the writer, and the critic of this world to show for all their wisdom? Has not God made the wisdom of this world look foolish? For it was after the world in its wisdom had failed to know God, that He in His wisdom chose to save all who would believe by the 'simple-mindedness' of the Gospel message. For the Jews ask for miraculous proofs and the Greeks an intellectual panacea, but *all we preach is Christ Crucified* — a stumbling block to the Jews and sheer nonsense to the Gentiles, but for those who are called, whether Jews or Greeks, (we preach) Christ the Power of God and the Wisdom of God. And this is really only natural, for God's 'foolishness' is wiser than men, and His 'weakness' is stronger than men." [4]

Paul refers here to two types of people who find the Gospel of the Cross particularly hard to swallow. In reality these two types include all men — as they are by nature. There are first of all the self-righteous. To them the Cross is nothing but a stumbling block. And then there are the worldly-wise. To them the Cross is sheer nonsense. Let's look at these two classes for just a moment.

First, the self-righteous. We shall have to admit that there was much in the first few chapters of

[4] *1 Corinthians 1:18-25.* P.

this book that went against the grain. The doctrine of the total depravity of the human heart is
anything but flattering. The natural heart resists,
denies, and rebels against such blanket indictments
of the Scriptures as: "There is no difference, for
*all* have sinned," [5] and, "There is not a just man
upon earth that doeth good and sinneth not." [6]
The natural heart will hear nothing of the Scriptural confessions: "We are all as an unclean thing,
and all our righteousnesses are as filthy rags," [7] or,
"I know that in me, that is, in my flesh, dwelleth
no good thing." [8] The natural heart just isn't ready
to give up and to exclaim with the Apostle Paul:
"O wretched man that I am! Who shall deliver me
from the body of this death?" [9]

The average man today is willing to admit, perhaps, that he isn't perfect, but somehow he thinks
he's good enough to get by. A few years ago we
were collaborating with a writer on the screenplay
for a full-length feature film. During our many
story sessions, which sometimes lasted far into the
night, we had frequent opportunity to speak of
the Biblical doctrine of sin and the Biblical message of salvation through the atonement of the
Savior. Months later our friend wrote and asked:
"While you were out here you kept talking about

[5] *Romans 3:22.*          [6] *Ecclesiastes 7:20.*
[7] *Isaiah 64:6.*          [8] *Romans 7:18.*
[9] *Romans 7:24.*

sin and salvation. I've been thinking a lot about what you said. But what I can't get through my head is — what have *I* done that calls for such a tremendous redemption?" He had not come to see that Sin was the controlling power of his life and that, unless freed from its guilt and curse and power by a firm reliance upon the message of the Cross, he would someday have to stand in the presence of God with no valid claim upon His mercy.

The message of the Cross, as we took great pains to point out in the early chapters of this book, is predicated upon the doctrine of the spiritual helplessness and hopelessness of man. It is predicated on the Scriptural doctrine that man, as he is by nature, is alienated from God [10] and that he can do nothing toward his own reconciliation and reinstatement into God's family.[11] That, to natural man, is an unmitigated affront. He wants no pass to heaven. He'll pay his own admission! He is sure that he is fully able. And so the Cross is to him a stumbling block, over which he falls to his own perdition.

The second class of people who cannot stomach the message of the Cross, says Paul, are the worldly-wise.[12] To them the Cross must be and remain "sheer nonsense." The superintellectual, the sophis-

---

[10] *Ephesians 2:12.*     [11] *Romans 3:19-28.*
[12] *1 Corinthians 1:18-25.*

ticate, the man who stubbornly insists that he will believe nothing which he is unable to explain, will never believe the Christian Gospel — at least not until the Holy Spirit has performed a miracle on his heart and replaced the stone of pride and disbelief with the seed of humble, trusting faith.

Let it be stated flatly, there is much about the Biblical message of the Cross that transcends human reason. Indeed, the Christian revelation brings up many questions which it does not answer. Any man who sets out to demonstrate the mysteries of the Atonement by an algebraic formula or by a logical syllogism is bound to get into difficulty. Any man who tries to answer all the questions which are posed by the doctrine of God's *justice* on the one hand and His *love* on the other is bound to run his head into a wall. The Christian revelation, as it were, is but a peek through a small hole in the curtain of eternity. Or, expressed with a little less elegance, it is only a knothole in a big board fence. In relation to the whole panorama which is on the other side, we can see only a little. But God in His wisdom has placed the Cross into our line of vision — in front of the hole through which we now are looking. That is what He wants us to see now. When the fence is taken down, we'll see a lot more, and many of the questions which now go begging for an answer will find their full reply.

Paul was not speaking specifically of the message of the Cross when he wrote the following words, but we shall not be doing them violence if we repeat them here. "At present," he says, ". . . we are like men looking at a landscape in a small mirror. The time will come when we shall see reality whole and face to face! At present all I know is a little fraction of the truth, but the time will come when I shall know it as fully as God now knows me." [13] This is not to say that the fundamental facts concerning the Cross of Christ and its redeeming purpose are not clearly stated in the Bible. These facts are as clear as the Empire State Building on a sunny day. But this is to say, rather, that many of the unanswered questions which cluster around the Bible's message of salvation will have to await their full and final answer until we reach the other side.

It is the refusal of the worldly-wise to accord their respective places to reason and revelation which causes them to recoil from the message of the Cross. They insist on understanding all or nothing. And so to them the Cross remains "sheer nonsense." [14] In the first chapter of his First Letter to the Corinthians, which we quoted earlier in this

[13] *1 Corinthians 13:12. P.*       [14] *1 Corinthians 1:23.*

chapter, Paul has a little more to say about the
worldly-wise and their attitude toward the Gospel
message. "For look at your own calling as Christians," he says. "You don't see among you many
of the wise (according to this world's judgment)
nor many of the ruling class nor many from the
noblest families. But God has chosen what the
world calls foolish to shame the wise; He has chosen
what the world calls weak to shame the strong
. . . that no man may boast in the presence of
God. . . . In the same way, my brothers, when
I came to proclaim to you God's secret purpose,
I did not come equipped with any brilliance of
speech or intellect. You may as well know now
that it was my secret determination to concentrate
entirely on Jesus Christ Himself and the fact of
His death upon the cross." [15] Paul came to the
pagan world of his day not with a complete and
well-rounded philosophy which would tickle the
intellects of the learned few, but with the simple
but powerful message of a great historical fact —
"Jesus Christ Himself and the fact of His death
upon the cross."

To the self-righteous that fact must always be
a stumbling block. To the worldly-wise it must be
sheer nonsense. But notice, Paul mentions a third
class. "But unto us which are saved, it is the *power*

[15] *1 Corinthians 1:26—2:2. P.*

*of God!*" [16] Whom does he mean by "us which are
saved"? He means that great multitude of men,
women, and children in all generations who, by
the power of the Holy Spirit, have believed the
simple Gospel message. To them the preaching of
the Cross is indeed the power of God, breaking the
shackles of Sin and Death and ushering them into
a newness of life which is beyond the grasp of
those who insist on clinging to their disbelief.[17]
To the Romans Paul writes: "I am not ashamed of
the Gospel of Christ, for it is the power of God
unto salvation to everyone that believeth." [18] What
is a stumbling block to some and rank foolishness
to others is the power of God unto salvation to
those who believe.

One need but look down the pages of history
to see this power of God at work. It was the power
of the Cross that turned the world upside down
during the early Christian era. It was the power
of the Cross which down through the centuries
rescued men from the tyranny of Sin and lifted
them into the freedom of the sons of God. And it
is the power of the Cross today which is reaching
down into the world's darkness and bringing bruised
and broken men up into His marvelous light.[19]

Remember, the human heart, as it is by nature,
is occupied territory. It is occupied by the despots

[16] *1 Corinthians 1:18.*        [17] *1 Corinthians 2:7-10.*
[18] *Romans 1:16.*        [19] *1 Peter 2:9.*

Sin and Death. No power on earth can ever unseat those tyrants from their throne. Small wonder, then, that when Paul by divine inspiration learned the true purpose and power of Christ's Cross, he should say: "I am not ashamed of the Gospel of Christ, for it is the power of *God* — the power of God *unto salvation,* to everyone that believeth." Here was the only power that could rescue humankind from the infernal shackles which held men in their grip!

Nonsense? Only to those who would have it so.

## XVI

## THE CROSS AND THE CHURCH

The Bible uses the word "church" in more than one sense. In its highest sense, the church is the total number of people throughout the world who have put their faith in the Biblical message of the Cross. They are the people who have been brought by God's Holy Spirit to the horrifying realization that their heart is indeed occupied territory, subject to the rule of Sin and Death. But they have also been moved by the Spirit of God to put their faith completely in the redeeming and emancipating power of the Cross of Christ. Whether they live in Chicago, London, Moscow, or Madrid, in the Fiji Islands, New Guinea, or Rangoon, whether their skin is black or white or red or yellow — if, under the Spirit's power, they have responded to the message of the Cross, they are part of the church in its highest sense.[1] This church is universal, transcending all bounds of

[1] *Ephesians 2:12-22.*

geography, of race or color or class. It is made up of all believers — but *only* believers.

The Bible also speaks of the church in a somewhat different sense. When, for instance, it refers to "the churches of Galatia" [2] or "the churches of Asia," [3] it is using the word in the sense of local groups of believers, that is, of congregations. That is perhaps the sense in which the average man today uses the word "church" most frequently. He thinks of the church in terms of people he knows — the church at the corner of Main and Elm, for instance. Without going into any technical discussion of the matter, let us point out one great difference between the church universal referred to in the paragraph above and the church at the corner of Main and Elm. The church universal is made up of believers only. The church down the street could, conceivably, include among its membership some who have never come to a real, living faith in Christ and His Cross. It is possible that within its membership there are some who are merely joiners. These people are as much a part of the church in the highest sense of the word as the mud on the wheel is part of the wagon. They may have joined, but they don't belong.

For obvious reasons, the ordinary man who has not given much thought to matters of religion finds

[2] *Galatians 1:2.*     [3] *1 Corinthians 16:19.*

it difficult to speak of any relationship whatever between himself and the Christian Church universal. What could he conceivably have in common with a group of believers in the islands of the South Pacific? Or what could he possibly have against them? But he *is* conscious of some relationship between himself and the church at the corner of Main and Elm. He is either a part of it, or he is not. In either case, there *is* a relationship. He is either in or out.

And there is also a relationship toward him which exists in the minds of the good people at Main and Elm. Regardless of what the nonreligious man may think, there *is* a relationship between the Christian congregation down the street and him. And that relationship has been established by the Cross of Christ. Christ has directed His followers to tell the nonreligious man about the message of His Cross. And there is nothing in all the world that the nonreligious man needs more. The church down the street, then, lives in a relationship of obligation to the nonreligious man, while he, in turn, lives in a relationship of need.

Anyone who has read the previous chapters of this book will understand why the church regards it as an unmitigated tragedy for any man to remain outside the circle of believers — outside the number of those who have been unshackled from the slavery of Sin and Death by the power of the Cross. The church regards it as its chief mission to proclaim spiritual deliverance to the spiritually captive. That is the directive of her Master.[4] The church looks upon all men, common or uncommon, as "sold under sin," [5] as being in spiritual bondage, as being alienated from God, "having no hope, and without God in the world." [6] There is no need to mince words; if you have not accepted the salvation of the Cross, the Christian congregation at the corner of Main and Elm looks upon you as still being occupied by the despots Sin and Death and in dire need of spiritual deliverance. It sees you as part of that tragic mass of humanity which is involved in "the Human Predicament" described in Chapter IV. It sees you as part of the universal parade, inexorably regimented into the cosmic death march, from which you can be delivered only by the emancipating power of the Cross, which the church has been commissioned to preach until the end of time.

Unfortunately the common man who is still outside the circle of believers doesn't seem to have caught on to the fact that that is what the church really thinks of him. There seems to be a widespread illusion that all good people and the church

---

[4] *Mark 16:15, 16.*       [5] *Romans 7:14.*
[6] *Ephesians 2:12.*

are on the same side, that all good people, both
within and without the church, are agreed on their
broad objectives. The fact is that in their broad
objectives the good people inside the church are
in perfect disagreement with the good people on
the outside. The good people on the inside are
out to rescue those on the outside and to give them
entirely new objectives. The good people on the
inside have a message for those on the outside and,
as long as they remain faithful to their trust, they
will continue to preach that message "in season and
out of season." [7]

It is only natural that those on the outside should
find it difficult to understand the church's preoccupation with the message of the Cross. And yet this
preoccupation should not be considered strange.
Think for a moment who these believers are. Having been delivered from the fearful power of Sin
and Death, they are bent on bringing this deliverance to others. Having been reconciled to God by
the death of His Son, they are bent on bringing all
men into this blessed state of reconciliation. Listen
to Paul as he establishes the relationship between
the message of the Cross and the purpose of the
church. "God was in Christ," he says, "reconciling
the world unto Himself, not imputing their trespasses unto them; and *hath committed unto us the*

[7] *2 Timothy 4:2.*

*Word of Reconciliation.* Now, then, we are ambassadors for Christ, as though God did beseech you
by us; we pray you, in Christ's stead, be ye reconciled to God!" [8] The church collectively, and the
believers individually, are ambassadors of Christ.
They have been entrusted with a message, a message addressed to the common man — to every man.
And the message? The message of reconciliation
through the Cross.

The trouble, of course, is that relatively few
people today look upon the church as an institution
with a supernatural message. (And the message of
the Cross surely *is* supernatural!) They regard
the church as a community institution, dedicated
to the cultivation of better and cleaner living. And,
as such, they regard it as an institution which all
public-spirited citizens should "get behind." They
send their children to its Sunday school, they give
discounts on the materials which it buys, they donate
cakes for its bake sales, potholders for its bazaars,
soda for its picnics, and perhaps even a substantial
check for its building fund. The church is doing
a fine job, and they want to have a part in it. Sometimes we wonder what these public-spirited citizens
would say if someone told them exactly what the
church's business is — where *they* fit into its "business." The church owes it to the common man who

[8] *2 Corinthians 5:19, 20.*

has not yet come to a vital faith in the Cross of Christ to tell him exactly what the church's message is. He needs the church's message much more than the church needs his favors.

One of the greatest dangers confronting the church today is its growing popularity — particularly its popularity among those who have never accepted its central message. In many cases the church has been hugged into silence by the smothering embrace of an unbelieving world. The world has said so many times that it agrees with the church that the church has been hypnotized into believing that it agrees with the world. The fact is that the church and the world can *never* agree. The central message of the church, the Cross, is an affront to the natural mind. Paul speaks of "the offense of the Cross." [9] The Cross is, and must forever remain, an offense to the unconverted heart. Only the divine surgery of the Spirit of God can effectively alter that.

Both the church and its unconverted neighbors will have to be awakened to the true relationship which has been established between them by the Cross of Jesus Christ. On the part of the church it is a relationship of solemn obligation. On the part of the unconverted neighbor it is a relationship of desperate need. A few paragraphs back we referred

[9] *Galatians 5:11.*

to the entire human race as being hopelessly regimented into a cosmic death march, headed inevitably toward its own destruction. If that is true — and that is the clear teaching of Christian revelation — then the church might be described as those who, by God's grace, have been ripped from the ranks of the marchers and who are now running alongside of the procession, offering a similar release to all who will accept it. In the language of Scripture, the church is the fellowship of the redeemed, proclaiming redemption to those who are still in spiritual bondage.

To the common man who is still outside its spiritual fellowship the church has this to say: "You are in desperate need! You are in need of the spiritual deliverance which only Christ can give you. You are in need of the release from Sin and Death which Christ has won for you through His death upon the cross. You are in need, urgent need, of the message of salvation which Christ has entrusted to His church."

# XVII

## YESTERDAY, TODAY, AND FOREVER

No presentation of the Cross of Christ would be complete without a clear statement of its *timelessness*. While it is true that the crucifixion of Christ took place on a specific day in human history, it is also true that the decision that there would have to be a Cross was made before the world's creation. It would be wrong to think of the Cross as a divine afterthought. It would be wrong to think of the Cross as a measure which God resorted to at a certain point in human history to make the best of a bad situation. The fact is, the Cross of Christ was an established fact in the mind of God before the sun, the moon, and the stars were rolled into their places. Man's redemption was fully planned before man ever made his first appearance.

Now, we shall readily admit that the above paragraph sounds somewhat abstruse and quite irrelevant, not to say presumptuous. Who *knows* what was in the mind of God before creation? And, after all, what difference does it make — except perhaps for the technical theologian? In answer to the first question, we say: God knows what was in His mind before the world's creation, and He has taken us into His confidence in the sacred pages of His revelation.[1] And in answer to the second question we say: It makes all the difference in the world for the alarmed and penitent sinner to know that God's plan of salvation for him is like a rainbow vaulting over the narrow span of time, with both ends rooted firmly in the two eternities — the eternity that is "past" and the eternity that is "future." The redemption of the penitent is more sure than the air which he breathes, the earth on which he walks, or the sunrise and the sunset by which he measures time. His redemption has its hinges in a timeless past, and it opens up into a timeless future.

But is there any Biblical basis for the assertion that the Cross and the entire plan of redemption was settled in the mind of God before the world began? Let's listen to Paul as he opens his Letter to the Christians at Ephesus: "Praise be to God," he says, "for giving us every possible spiritual benefit in Christ! For consider what He has done!

[1] *1 Corinthians 2:11-13.*

*Before the foundation of the world* He chose us to become, in Christ, His holy and blameless children living within His constant care." [2] The Scriptures also speak clearly of the "grace which was given us in Christ Jesus *before the world began.*" [3] And the Apostle Peter told the Christians of Asia Minor that they had been redeemed from Sin and Death "not with silver and gold . . . but with the precious blood of Christ, as of a lamb without blemish and without spot, who verily was fore-ordained *before the foundation of the world,* but was manifest in these last times for you who by Him do believe in God." [4] There can be no doubt at all that the Bible asserts that the Cross was a fact in the mind of God already before the world's creation.

It is significant, however, that whenever the Bible speaks of the Cross of Christ as having been in the mind and heart of God already before the beginning of time, it is addressing the *believer.* It presents this doctrine not as an intellectual proposition for the unbeliever to debate, but rather as a divine fact for the believer to accept for his comfort and assurance. Whenever the believer thinks of God, he is to think of Him in terms of Christ. And whenever he thinks of Christ, he is

[2] *Ephesians 1:3-10. P.*       [3] *2 Timothy 1:9.*
[4] *1 Peter 1:19-21.*

to think of Him in terms of His Cross. And whenever he thinks of the Cross, he is to think of it in terms of God's eternity. The Cross and its divine purpose and its divine power were there for him — already before the beginning of time. Indeed, if he is a believer in Christ, he may rest assured that, already before the world began, God chose him individually as one of His redeemed,[5] not because of any merit of his own but solely because of the Cross of Christ.

The importance of this part of the Christian revelation can hardly be overemphasized. The message of the Cross is, as it were, a *line* in time on which the entire history of man on earth is only a *point*. The message was here before man. And it will continue long after man's little day on this planet will have ended. What the Scriptures say of Jesus Himself can also be said of the purpose and the power and the glory of His Cross: "Jesus Christ the same yesterday and today and forever!" [6] As He is eternal and unchanging, so, too, is the power of His Cross. The sinner who has come to the brink of despair because of his transgression can know that when he puts his confidence in the Cross of Christ, he has fastened his anchor into the moorings of eternity. Such an assurance is

---

[5] *Ephesians 1:4, 5.*        [6] *Hebrews 13:8.*

beyond the change and decay of time. It knows
"no change nor variableness." It has placed its
feet — outside of time — on the solid bedrock of
God's eternity.

> On Christ, the solid Rock, I stand;
> All other ground is sinking sand.

But if it is true that the message of the Cross
is rooted in eternity "*past,*" it is also true that its
message will echo and re-echo throughout eternity
"*future.*" Its message was determined before the
world began, and it will continue after the world
has ended. The Apostle John wrote the last book of
the Bible while in exile on the Isle of Patmos. In
this book, known as "The Revelation of St. John the
Divine," he records a series of prophetic visions. In
his seventh chapter he describes a marvelous vision
of heaven, in which he saw "a great multitude, which
no man could number, of all nations and kindreds
and people and tongues," who "stood before the
throne and before the Lamb, clothed with white
robes, and palms in their hands." In reply to the
question: "What are these which are arrayed in
white robes? And whence came they?" an elder
gives the answer: "These are they which came out
of great tribulation, and have washed their robes
and made them white in the blood of the Lamb. . . .
They shall hunger no more, neither thirst any more;
neither shall the sun light on them nor any heat.

For the Lamb which is in the midst of the throne shall feed them and shall lead them unto living fountains of waters; and God shall wipe away all tears from their eyes." [7]

John tells us that he saw the redeemed of all nations gathered around the Lamb. And who are these redeemed? "They are they . . . which have washed their robes and made them white in the blood of the Lamb." Here in the eternal presence of Christ we see those who have found refuge in the message of His Cross. Here we see those who on earth accepted the divine invitation of their Lord: "Come now, and let us reason together, saith the Lord: though your sins be as scarlet, they shall be as white as snow; though they be red like crimson, they shall be as wool," [8] and who put their trust in the assurance that "the blood of Jesus Christ, His Son, cleanseth us from all sin." [9] Here we see the final fulfillment of the "divine mystery" of which we wrote at length in Chapter VII, the mystery of complete and unconditional pardon through the substitution of a lamb — spelled with a small "l" in the Old Testament and with a capital in the New. The Lamb on the throne in heaven is none other than the Lamb who walked the dusty roads of Palestine during the days of His flesh and whom John

[7] *Revelation 7:9-17.*        [8] *Isaiah 1:18.*
[9] *1 John 1:7.*

the Baptist hailed as "the Lamb of God which taketh away the sin of the world." [10] The Lamb who died on a wooden cross by the decree of Pontius Pilate is both "the Lamb slain from the foundation of the world" [11] and "the Lamb which is in the midst of the throne." [12] Christ is the Lamb — yesterday and today and forever. The message of the Cross is indeed a glorious, reassuring rainbow, arching across all human history, from eternity East to eternity West.

There is, of course, a very practical side to the doctrine which we've been handling in this chapter. Have you ever felt that the world had gone crazy and you were going crazy with it — that nothing made sense any more — that all of life was a purposeless jumble? Have you ever felt that you were nothing but a speck of dust in a whirlwind — tossed hither and yon by the whims of fate? Have you ever felt that God had vacated His heavens and that you had been left dreadfully alone? Have you ever become thoroughly convinced that God, if there *is* a God, has completely forgotten you?

The message of the Cross tells you that God had you in His mind already in eternity past — before the foundations of the world were laid. And it tells you that God wants to have you at His side

10 *John 1:29.*        11 *Revelation 13:8.*
12 *Revelation 7:17.*

throughout eternity future — after the foundations of this world are shattered forever. Before the world began, He determined to send His Son into the world to redeem you so that you could live with Him in the endless glories of His heaven. Yes, you were the object of His concern before your mother knew you, and He wants to keep you the object of His concern long after your name has been forgotten on this earth. Yesterday and today and forever the Cross is the revelation of God's eternal purpose, the purpose of His *love*.

## XVIII

## SONGS OF THE CROSS

We were called to the bed of an elderly woman who lay dying in a hospital. Although unable to speak, she was fully conscious. Knowing her to be a sincere believer, we quoted to her those passages of the Bible which seemed to be particularly applicable to the moment. There was John Three, verse sixteen: "God so loved the world." There was John Fourteen, two: "In My Father's house are many mansions . . . I go to prepare a place for you." And John Eleven, twenty-five: "I am the Resurrection and the Life." She listened attentively and, we would say, appreciatively; but for some reason or other it seemed that we had not found that responsive chord in her heart which we had touched so frequently before. She stared expressionless toward the ceiling, her arms lying limp on the bed beside her.

We then quoted a number of familiar hymn stanzas — stanzas which she had learned in her childhood. Suddenly her eyes moistened, and it was evident that she was weeping tears of joy. Her weak arms moved, and she folded her hands across her breast. The chambers of her dying heart were filled with meaningful music as she breathed heavenward the familiar words which we were speaking:

> Rock of Ages, cleft for me,
> Let me hide myself in Thee.
>> Let the water and the blood
>> From Thy riven side which flowed
> Be of sin the double cure,
> Cleanse me from its guilt and power.

There was a glow of victory on her face, as though she had already turned the corner and were looking up a bright and shining staircase which we, who lingered behind, could not see. She was going where, for the moment, we could not follow. But as she went, she seemed to smile as she heard us repeat all the words of that glorious hymn:

> Not the labors of my hands
> Can fulfill Thy Law's demands;
>> Could my zeal no respite know,
>> Could my tears forever flow,
> All for sin could not atone;
> Thou must save, and Thou alone!

Nothing in my hand I bring,
Simply to Thy CROSS I cling;
    Naked, come to Thee for dress;
    Helpless, look to Thee for grace;
Foul, I to the fountain fly;
Wash me, Savior, or I die!

While I draw this fleeting breath,
When my eyelids close in death,
    When I soar to worlds unknown,
    See Thee on Thy judgment throne,
Rock of Ages, cleft for me,
Let me hide myself in Thee!

Millions upon millions have left this world, breathing the inexpressible thoughts which lie between the lines of our Christian hymns. For it is there, above and beneath the lines of our truly Christian hymnody, that the human heart finds some of its purest and most sublime theology. Surely, all of us have learned that there are some thoughts which the human mind is incapable of framing and which the human tongue is incapable of uttering. The young man, for instance, who is deeply in love soon finds mere prose hopelessly inadequate to express the feelings of his heart, and so he resorts to poetry. Poetry, as it were, adds a new dimension to his words, a dimension which is limited in its extent only by the reach of his imagination — a dimension which is far beyond the gravity-pull of mere language.

And so, too, it is with the love of God to man as revealed by the Cross of Christ, and the love of man to God which flows back to Him in response to that Cross. It simply cannot be contained in those puny little cups which we humans call words; it is bound to spill over. And experience has shown that the first place it spills is from prose to poetry. Who can ever count the hundreds of thousands of hymns that have been written in an effort to give expression to the inexpressible implications of the Cross of Christ! Again and again these hymns have added a dimension to our experience which would have been unutterable in prose. Take, for instance, the well-known hymn which we quoted only a moment ago. A thick volume could be written on the very first two lines of Toplady's immortal poem:

> Rock of Ages, cleft for me,
> Let me hide myself in Thee!

In those two lines, with their overtones and undertones, we have the entire message of the Cross. And we have it expressed with such picturesqueness that the mind is fairly flooded with pictures, all of them, as it were, interpretations and applications of the message of the Cross.

We have never traveled through Arizona and New Mexico on the Santa Fe without thinking of these first two (and last two!) lines of Toplady's hymn. Rising high above the surrounding prairie,

almost perpendicular, are ranges of rocky mountains — a veritable wilderness of stone. As the train
winds through this wild and rugged labyrinth, one
can see an occasional smooth, deep crevice riven
far into the mountainside. It would seem that
nature had cleft the rock to provide a place of
refuge and security for mountain animals and for
men who might be caught in raging mountain
storms.

What a picture of Christ — and His Cross! "Rock
of Ages, cleft for me, Let me hide myself in Thee!"
Scripture frequently refers to God as a Rock, a Rock
of Refuge and Strength.[1] Indeed, in one passage it
calls Him "the Rock of Ages." [2] That Rock was
cleft and became a refuge for all mankind when
Christ died upon the Cross. Anyone who hides in
the cleft Rock of Ages has found security against
all his spiritual enemies — Sin, Death, Satan, and
Hell. The crucified Christ is the sinner's only
Refuge.

But the poet also had another picture in mind.
At one time, when the Children of Israel were wan-
dering through the wilderness, there was an acute
shortage of water. The Lord told Moses to smite
a certain rock and promised that refreshing water
would flow from it. Moses obeyed the Lord and

---

[1] *Psalm 94:22.*      [2] *Isaiah 26:4.*

found that His promise was true.[3] In the New
Testament Paul gives this incident a spiritual in-
terpretation when he says: "They all shared the
same spiritual food and drank the same spiritual
drink, for they drank from the spiritual Rock which
followed them, and that Rock was Christ."[4] In
other words, just as the cleft rock was a source of
refreshment and strength in a *physical* sense to the
wanderers in the desert, so the cleft Rock, which
was Christ, was to be a source of refreshment and
strength and healing in a *spiritual* sense. It was
this picture in the mind of the poet which prompted
the lines:

> Let the water and the blood
> From Thy riven side which flowed
> Be of sin the double cure,
> Cleanse me from its guilt and power.

and the lines:

> Foul, I to the fountain fly;
> Wash me, Savior, or I die.

When the Rock of Ages was cleft for all mankind,
that is, when the Son of God gave His life on a cross
for the sins of the world, there was opened up, as
it were, an eternal spring from which flow streams
of healing and forgiveness. For "the blood of Jesus
Christ, His Son, cleanseth us from all sin."[5] May
we suggest that you turn back a page or two now

---

[3] *Exodus 17:6.*     [4] *1 Corinthians 10:4. P.*
[5] *1 John 1:7.*

and read Toplady's entire hymn slowly, reverently, prayerfully, and see how the white spaces between the lines fairly *shout* the theology of the Cross.

When we were a little boy, our mother taught us to pray an old German hymn stanza every night before we went to sleep. The stanza has suffered considerably in translation, but it ran something like this:

> Jesus, Thy blood and righteousness,
> My beauty are, my glorious dress,
> Wherein before my God I'll stand
> When I shall reach the heavenly land.

Now, technical theologians will tell us that the first line of that stanza has to do with the passive and active obedience of Christ (developed in our Chapters XIII and IX). They will tell us that the second line has to do with the imputed righteousness of the Savior, of which we also spoke previously in this volume. And they will be *right*. But how much more fraught with meaning and comfort and inspiration and strength are the words just as they read! The child or the man or the woman who prays that prayer from the bottom of his heart steps into the presence of his Maker, not pointing to his own merit or achievement, but trusting in the "blood and righteousness of Christ." In Christ's blood he has found atonement for all his sin, and in Christ's righteousness he has found a garment which covers all his guilt. These are the gorgeous finery in which someday he will stand before his God. These (the blood and righteousness of Christ) comprise the "wedding garment" which God provides for every sinner who steps into His presence, pleading the merits of the Savior. These comprised the righteousness which enabled Paul to look forward to death confidently saying: "Not having mine *own* righteousness . . . but that which is through the faith of Christ." [6]

To the man who finds the Christian message of the Cross too technical, too theological, or perhaps even irrelevant to the burning issues of life today, we say: read the great treasury of Christian hymns, and see what the message of the Cross has meant to some of the noblest men and women of history.

There is much, very much, about the Gospel of the Cross that can never be put into words. He who has once been touched by its power will have utterly new dimensions of experience, which he will find it difficult to share. Some things he shall never be able adequately to explain to those who are not yet looking at the Cross through the eyes of faith. But explain them or not, he has no doubt as to their validity. He has been assured of their validity by the written promise of his God, the inspired Scriptures.

[6] *Philippians 3:9.*

The Apostle Paul was speaking of the unexplain-ableness of the Cross when he told his Corinthian Christians: "Eye hath not seen, nor ear heard, neither have entered the heart of man, the things which God hath prepared for them that love Him. But God hath revealed them unto us by His Spirit." [7] Paul is here not referring to a future experience in heaven. He is referring to an experience here and now. What he is saying is simply this: Those who have taken the miracle of the Cross into their hearts are in for an experience which has, otherwise, never entered the head or heart of man. Small wonder, then, that the church of all ages has given wings to its words and has soared the heights of poetry to extol the grandeurs of the Cross. It was a man who had viewed the Cross of Christ from the bottom of the valley of disillusionment who wrote more than two hundred years ago:

Oh, that I had a thousand voices!
　　A mouth to speak with thousand tongues!
My heart, which in the Lord rejoices,
　　Then would proclaim in grateful songs
To all, wherever I might be,
　　What great things God hath done for me.

The church has sung for two thousand years. And the reason for its songs has been the Cross!

[7] *1 Corinthians 2:2-10.*

## THE WONDROUS CROSS

When I survey the wondrous Cross
   On which the Prince of Glory died,
My richest gain I count but loss
   And pour contempt on all my pride.

Forbid it, Lord, that I should boast
   Save in the death of Christ, my God;
All the vain things that charm me most,
   I sacrifice them to His blood.

Were the whole realm of nature mine,
   That were a tribute far too small;
Love so amazing, so divine,
   Demands my soul, my life, my all!

ISAAC WATTS